"Pillars of Greatness—Isaac Principle is bold and incisive. This is a book that will be read and talked about for years because it dares to be practical without losing the flavor of the Word of God."

Pastor James Fadele,
Chairman Board of Coordinators
The Redeemed Christian Church of God North America

PILLARS *of*
GREATNESS

Isaac Principles

1 Cor. 2:9

PILLARS *of* GREATNESS

Isaac Principles

TAYO OJAJUNI

TATE PUBLISHING & *Enterprises*

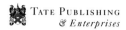

TATE PUBLISHING
& Enterprises

Tate Publishing is committed to excellence in the publishing industry. Our staff of highly trained professionals, including editors, graphic designers, and marketing personnel, work together to produce the very finest books available. The company reflects the philosophy established by the founders, based on Psalms 68:11,

"THE LORD GAVE THE WORD AND GREAT WAS THE COMPANY OF THOSE WHO PUBLISHED IT."

If you would like further information, please contact us:
1.888.361.9473 | www.tatepublishing.com
TATE PUBLISHING & Enterprises, LLC | 127 E. Trade Center Terrace
Mustang, Oklahoma 73064 USA

I dedicate this book to my Lord and Savior Jesus Christ for bringing me out of the miry clay and setting my feet on the Rock to stay. Also, to my lovely wife Bunmi and our wonderful children, Tobi, Mowa and Timi. Thanks for always being there.

ACKNOWLEDGEMENTS

I want to thank my daddy in the Lord, Pastor E. A. Adeboye, for taking the time to not only go through this book, but also to write a foreword. Also, thanks to his wife and mummy in the Lord Pastor Foluke Adeboye.

Without a doubt I give thanks to the chairman of the board of coordinators of The Redeemed Christian Church of God North America, Pastor James Fadele.

I appreciate the candid observations, corrections and diligence of the following: Sola Balogun, Tunji Ishola, Kunle Fafiolu and Wilson Muzorewa during the putting together of this manuscript. You are indeed co-laborers in the Lord.

The vessels that God used as a conduit for me to come to the earth are special, and I am very grateful to you, Chief and Mrs. Martins Mobolaji Ojajuni.

For all the members of The Redeemed Christian Church of God Covenant Chapel in Toronto Canada, I express my appreciation.

COMMENT

The foundation of a pillar determines the kind of structure it will support. For Paul of Tarsus, his pillar was formed on the way to Damascus—his was a pillar of solid foundation when he said, "Lord, what wilt thou have me to do?" For Abraham, his pillar was established when he obeyed God's command and departed from his home country—his was a foundation of obedience! Isaac continued in the same stead as he obediently surrendered to be made a sacrifice for the God of his father, Abraham.

With this extraordinarily candid debut, author and former Information Technology professional Pastor Tayo Ojajuni, a shepherd of the Lord's flock in Toronto, Canada, takes his place beside those in a long eminent tradition of spiritual authors. *Pillars of Greatness–Isaac Principles* is bold and incisive. This is a book that will be read and talked about for years because it dares to be practical without losing the flavor of the Word of God.

Once you recognize yourself as a "child of promise," then step up by *initiating* something; you've got to sow before you can reap an *increase!* Challenges would come, but knowing that you are a joint heir with our Lord Jesus Christ, be rest assured that He will bring you out.

The nuggets at the end of each chapter would serve you as desserts, and then you seal the learning points with the prayers. This is not mere literature; it is designed to speak to your heart and edify your Spirit. This book shall become a classic in Jesus' name!

Bravo, Pastor Tayo Ojajuni. More anointing in Jesus' name!

–Pastor James Fadele

TABLE OF CONTENTS

FOREWORD

Metaphorically, in *"Pillars of Greatness–Isaac Principles,"* Tayo Ojajuni has painstakingly shown how tons of sand, gravel and steel can become a magnificent skyscraper. These raw materials are put together in the right ratio, place, form, shape and time by exploiting their properties and characteristics, strength and flexibility. It takes right timing and precise positioning. It takes skill and discipline. It takes hard work, diligence and perseverance. Properly done, the pillars will emerge and hold.

The building materials of life are available to everyone. God has assured that, but very few mold these raw materials into pillars of a great life. The author draws deeply on God's Word to help every Christian reach his potential in Christ Jesus. The sage's words have also been put to good effect. I used to, for instance, describe opportunity as a man with lots of hair in front of his head but bald at the back. The only way to catch opportunity, therefore, is to grab him by the front as he approaches. If you ever let him go by, then you have lost him. Try as you might, you cannot catch him from the rear. Of course you have heard the well-known saying "opportunity knocks only once." Tayo Ojajuni quotes Thomas Edison on opportunity: "lots of people miss opportunity because it is covered in overalls and looks like work." Work, physical and mental, is an integral part of opportunity. The point is well made in this book.

As you take full advantage of the opportunity to read this book, new insights into the deep meaning and application of the Word of God will open a vista to you. The nuggets at the end of every chapter condense great wisdom and truth into simple, easy-to-remember phrases or sentences. Of course the prayer points that follow pull down divine assistance in this very important endeavor.

This book will help you turn the specific raw materials God made available to you into a great meaningful life.

I recommend this book to anyone who is determined to make the best use of all God has made available to him or her and who is preparing to give a good account on the day of the Lord.

God bless you as you read.
Pastor E. A. Adeboye

INTRODUCTION

Every individual aspires to be great. You can say, "Wait a minute, I am a quiet and modest person." Okay, but in whatever you do, you still want to excel. When you tower or rise above your compatriots, there is a measure of greatness. All you want could be to get a good job and keep it, excel in your exams, have a good home, be healed from a disease, etc. These are all types of greatness. One thing that is absolutely sure is that greatness is relative.

While some will want to rule the world—and to them that defines greatness—another may just want to be a philanthropist. The most important thing is that whatever you start to do according to divine direction, do it well.

In the quest to be great, there are backbones, catalysts, or supports. These could be animate or inanimate. It could even be a disappointment. In some cases, it may be a friend or foe. All these when put together and used positively become pillars.

A physical pillar could be visible or invisible. It all depends on design, or the architect. In some bridges built by a technology called suspension, the pillars are "in the air" and very much visible while you are driving across the bridge. In some other bridges, the pillars are below. Also, in some buildings, especially large halls or auditoriums, you will see thick columns, and in some others you will not see any.

If you want a building or structure to crumble, go for the pillars. During the September 11, 2001 strike on the World Trade Center towers, the buildings imploded easily and quickly because the high heat from the plane explosion melted the steel beams that were the pillars, and the buildings crumbled within minutes of each other.

A LOOK AT SAMSON

And Samson said unto the lad that held him by the hand, Suffer me that I may feel the pillars whereupon the house standeth, that I may lean upon them. Now the house was full of men and women; and all the lords of the Philistines were there; and there were upon the roof about three thousand men and women, that beheld while Samson made sport. And Samson called unto the LORD, and said, O Lord God, remember me, I pray thee, and strengthen me, I pray thee, only this once, O God, that I may be at once avenged of the Philistines for my two eyes. And Samson took hold of the two middle pillars upon which the house stood, and on which it was borne up, of the one with his right hand, and of the other with his left. And Samson said, Let me die with the Philistines. And he bowed himself with all his might; and the house fell upon the lords, and upon all the people that were therein. So the dead which he slew at his death were more than they which he slew in his life.
(Judges 16: 26 -30, KJV)

Samson was a child consecrated unto the Lord from the womb. He did exploits for God, but he allowed the cares of the world to take pre-eminence. He was arrested, imprisoned, his two eyes were pulled from the sockets, and he became a laughing stock so much so that the victor became vanquished. On a particular day, he was released from prison so that he could be ridiculed, but he decided that enough was enough.

Samson asked to be taken close to the pillars of the building he was in. He moved close to the pillars of the building, pushed it down, and it crumbled. The building collapsed and killed all those in the building, including him. To destroy the building, Samson located the structure holding the building up and pushed it down.

Pillars are important structures in any entity. For any measure of greatness that an individual is enjoying or hopes to achieve, there are pillars either upholding the individual or that the individual needs to build up. Pillars hold the world.

> For the pillars of the earth are the LORD's, and He hath set the world upon them. (1 Samuel 2: 8, KJV)

> When the earth goes topsy-turvy and nobody knows which end is up, I nail it all down, I put everything in place again. (Psalm 75: 3, MSG)

> When the earth totters, and all the inhabitants of it, it is I Who will poise and keep steady its pillars. Selah [pause, and calmly think of that]! (Psalm 75: 3, TAB)

Without any iota of doubt, the "foundational pillar" that any individual needs to attain greatness is God. He is upholding everything, and He can change the course of anything. The earth is His, and the fullness thereof. The silver and the gold belongs unto Him, the riches in the secret places belong to Him. He knows the best way to be healed. He can raise up a beggar out of the dunghill, and with Him nothing shall be impossible.

Despite the importance of the "foundational pillar," as human beings we also need to build our "little" pillars of greatness on the foundational pillar.

THE MAN ISAAC

Then Isaac sowed in that land, and received in the same year a hundredfold: and the LORD blessed him. And the man waxed great, and went forward, and grew until he became very great: For he had possession of flocks, and possession of herds, and great store of servants: and the Philistines envied him. For all the wells which his father's servants had digged in the days of Abraham his father, the Philistines had stopped them, and filled them with earth. And Abimelech said unto Isaac, Go from us; for thou art much mightier than we. And Isaac departed thence, and pitched his tent in the valley of Gerar, and dwelt there. And Isaac digged again the wells of water, which they had digged in the days of Abraham his father; for the Philistines had stopped them after the death of Abraham: and he called their names after the names by which his father had called them. And Isaac's servants digged in the valley, and found there a well of springing water. And the herdmen of Gerar did strive with Isaac's herdmen, saying, The water is ours: and he called the name of the well Esek; because they strove with him. And they digged another well, and strove for that also: and he called the name of it Sitnah. And he removed from thence, and digged another well; and for that they strove not: and he called the name of it Rehoboth; and he said, For now the LORD hath made room for us, and we shall be fruitful in the land. (Genesis 26: 12–22, KJV)

Above is the story of the "first son" of Abraham. Isaac had very challenging, peculiar and special attributes. Below are some of them.

A covenant child—Genesis 17:9
A child of promise—Genesis 21:1
A child of old age—Genesis 21:5
An obedient child—Genesis 22: 8–9
A mocked child—Genesis 21:9
A loved child—Genesis 22:2
An only child—Genesis 22:2
A blessed child—Genesis 25:11
An intercessor—Genesis 25:21
A loving man—Genesis 26: 8
A sower—Genesis 26:12
A digger—Genesis 26:18

These attributes reveal some of the advantages and disadvantages that Isaac had. Looking at Isaac, it is possible to think that he had it made. Of course he was a child of Abraham and therefore blessed. As children of God, we are also blessed. The Word of God says that we have been blessed with all spiritual blessings in the heavenly realm because we belong to Christ.

We can say he had an inheritance by virtue of being the son of Abraham, but we are also a joint-heir with Christ. Isaac developed good behavior by himself, and he was not a slothful child. He was ridiculed by his step brother Ishmael, but he did not allow this to be a hindrance. At one time or the other, we have been ridiculed or jeered. Did we decide to lie low, roll over, and give up? Isaac was also an only child of his mother, but he did not use that as an excuse in his relational quotient. Isaac experienced lack, and what it means to be hungry. When you are in a situation of famine, if you have anything saved, you ration it because you do not know when the next meal is going to come. He knew what it meant to go to the ATM or the bank teller and have the response be "insufficient funds." At a time he wanted to relocate, which means he understood what dissatisfaction meant.

A major reason why all these attributes are being highlighted is to show that the challenges that we are facing, Isaac also faced. We are covenant children, for we are joined to Christ. We are no longer aliens to the covenant of promise; we are heirs of the Father, and joint heirs with Christ. We are peculiar people and a royal priesthood.

We have been blessed with all blessings in heavenly places. As Isaac when he was faced with famine decided to do something, we must also develop and entrench our pillars of greatness. There will always be challenges, but if you have the right pillars entrenched, you will always be a winner, a champion, and an overcomer. Isaac, despite famine, still had it in him to apply the power of joy. He did not neglect his home, and he had fun with his family.

God has destined you to be great, and you shall be great, and it shall be well with you. It is time to do something. The dough that hates the challenge of the oven will never experience the joy of rising up. A deep look at the life of Isaac in Genesis chapter 26 reveals that he did certain things to become great. These will be known as the eight pillars of greatness, or the Isaac principles, that will be discussed in this book. They are:

- Invest
- Increase
- Initiate
- Insight
- Insult (ill-will)
- Integrity
- Inquire
- Impact

As you continue to read, may the gift in you be stirred up in Jesus' mighty name, amen.

NUGGETS

- Every individual aspires to be great, but greatness is relative.
- A pillar can be a support or a catalyst depending on one's circumstance.
- A pillar could be visible or invisible.
- The life of Isaac, through his peaks and troughs, epitomizes even our lives as children of God in our pursuit of greatness.
- From the life of Isaac, we note that there are eight pillars of greatness, or Isaac Principles, namely: Invest; Increase; Initiate; Insight; Insult; Integrity; Inquire; Impact.

PRAYER POINTS

- My Father, establish your pillars of greatness in my life in Jesus' name.
- My God, you are my "foundational pillar." Let the building of my greatness forever remain strong.
- My Lord, build me up in greatness, in Jesus' name.
- My God, whatever may want to destroy what you are building in my life, destroy all such in Jesus' name.
- Oh Lord, make room for me. Make room for my greatness, in Jesus' name.
- Father, enlarge my coast.
- I know, Lord, that you have destined me to be great. Let my greatness start now.
- As a joint heir with Christ, I receive all things that pertain to life and godliness, to enable me to succeed and overcome, in Jesus' name.
- My God, the wisdom to be great give unto me in Jesus' name. Amen.
- Abba Father, make me great.

INVEST

Empty the coins of your purse into your mind and your mind will fill your purse with coins.

- Benjamin Franklin

...then Isaac sowed in that land. (Genesis 26: 12, KJV)

To sow means to propagate, spread or plant. Sowing requires effort. In the olden days, you had to plough the land using rudimentary implements, and if you were rich, you ploughed with yoke of oxen. Depending on how big your farm is, the seeds you plant can either be locally planted or broadcasted. No matter the style that you use, it still involves some degree of manual labor. The aim of the one who plants or sows is to reap. The person that is planting could have used the seed for other things (e.g. food), but he decided to invest the seed to make a profit. This implies that sowing is an investment that involves sacrifice. You forgo the now for the future; you use today to get tomorrow. In economics, we can say that the opportunity cost of the harvest that the sower hopes to reap is the alternative of consuming the seed that he forgoes.

For Isaac, the time he sowed was not convenient; it was a tough time. You cannot wait for a convenient time to do things that will yield fruit. An investment is a venture (nothing ventured, nothing gained), and it is also an asset. To invest means to put in (e.g. time, effort), spend, devote, advance (e.g. the cause of something). The word "invest" is a transitive verb.

In Medieval Latin, the word is called *investire,* i.e. to clothe, (*vestis* = garment). A cloth covers, so that when an individual is investing, he is covering famine, shame, hunger, reproach, poverty, nakedness, sorrow, etc. At that time in Gerar there was famine, but when Isaac started investing, he was not only covering poverty, but also shame. Remember that Isaac was a child of covenant living in a foreign land called Gerar. He would have boasted to the Gerarites about the powers of the God of Abraham, and he would also have mentioned the meaning of his name—laughter. When famine came, they would be asking him about that God who is great and mighty; asking if God is sleeping, or peradventure had gone on a journey. Isaac would have been immersed in ridicule, but investment turned him to amazement.

By investing, Isaac was also fulfilling the meaning of his name—laughter. Where there is famine, there cannot be laughter, but weeping (2Kings 6). Investing is not always convenient. Isaac invested the seed he had in a land that people thought was barren. Do not allow the thoughts of men debar you from taking the right step. The right step that you refuse to take will amount to the success that you did not make.

Any Godly investment is guaranteed to yield because the law of harvest cannot be contravened; "while the earth remain seedtime... and harvest shall not cease." A glorious revelation in this scripture is that while there is seedtime, there is no harvest time. In as much as you have sown, harvest will definitely follow continually. Harvest, according to the principle of the Word of God, is not limited to a particular time. A downpour of blessing can start when you least expect. You have crops that are annual, semiannual, perennial, etc. They have a life cycle; when you plant the seed of these crops, you have to wait for a particular time for it to grow (in some cases years). For Godly investment, the yield on investment can be anytime and anywhere. The harvest is always more than the seed sown. This is why the Word of God says goodness and mercy shall follow me all the days of my life.

To invest means to multiply, and this is tied to a commandment given to man. *"And God blessed them, and God said unto them, Be fruitful, and multiply"* (Genesis 1: 28, KJV).

Because God is a great God and desires greatness for his children, he said, "be fruitful and multiply," or to paraphrase in the context of this study—invest. God is a businessman and a wise investor. *"For God so loved the world that he gave his only Son, so that everyone who believes in him will not perish but have eternal life..."* (John 3: 16, NLT) He did this so that he will have more sons and daughters.

From John 3:16, you see the motive behind the investment—for God so *loved* the world. One thing that will guarantee an instant, delayed or denied return on any investment is the motive.

> [Or] you do ask [God for them] and yet fail to receive, because you ask with wrong purpose and evil, selfish motives. Your intention is [when you get what you desire] to spend it in sensual pleasures. (James 4: 3, TAB)

> And even when you do ask, you don't get it because your whole motive is wrong—you want only what will give you pleasure. (James 4: 3, NLT)

While God encourages investment, the heart, mind, purpose and objective of the investor will always be carefully scrutinized by God. For any investment, He is the only one that can guarantee an increase. There is somebody at the center of the process, and He is no other than Jehovah Elohim—the creator.

> It's not the one who plants or the one who waters who is at the center of this process but God, who makes things grow. (1 Corinthians 3: 7, MSG)

WHAT TO INVEST?

Time

This can be described as a non-spatial continuum in which events occur in apparently irreversible succession from the past through the present to the future. It can also be explained as a period or periods designated for a given activity.

-The American Heritage Dictionary of The English Language
by Houghton Mifflin Company

If you believe in it, you spend time on it. "*There is a time for everything, a season for every activity under heaven*" (Ecclesiastes 3: 1, NLT).

We must use our time wisely. Every individual is handed 24 hours each day. What we do with the 24 hours will determine what we are going to be. God values time; this is the reason you find him spending time with man in the Garden of Eden; coming down in the cool of the day.

Your life is shaped by your routine. Task management was instrumental to the appointment of the first set of deacons in the Bible. Task management ensures the wise use of ones time.

So the Twelve called a meeting of all the believers. "We apostles should spend our time preaching and teaching the Word of God, not administering a food program," they said. (Acts 6: 2, NLT)

A wonderful thing about the Most High God is the limit He has placed upon Himself, and the limit is that He cannot lie. As His children, we should also know our limits. As painful as it may sound, we do not have unlimited power. We should channel our energies and resources towards those things that will promote, project and propel us to our destiny. This principle is commonly known as the Pareto Effect, which states that we should focus our attention on the vital issues.

It is important in everything that we do in life that we should not try to be a jack-of-all-trades. Concentrated activity brings about concrete result. The apostles could have tried to do it all, and in the end they would have become worn out without achieving anything of significance. In an attempt to do it all, they would have been hailed by people that do not understand the concept of task management.

At a time, Jethro the Midianite (Moses' father-in-law) recognized the efficiency of Moses without any apparent effectiveness, and he had to caution him on the importance of task management.

> Moses' father-in-law replied, "What you are doing is not good. You and these people who come to you will only wear yourselves out. The work is too heavy for you; you cannot handle it alone. (Exodus 18: 17–18, NIV)

In both examples, you see the mentioning of "administering a food program" and "the work is too heavy for you." While time is fixed (24 hours per day), tasks are not fixed. Tasks can represent a variable in an equation. It makes sense to manage the tasks effectively. When this is done, time will become well-managed and available. Delegation of tasks is part of task management. There are some tasks that you need to delegate so that your worth can show forth. Maintaining balance enhances success. When you delegate tasks, you are also investing in the life of someone and fostering togetherness.

The Kenyan Kikuyu tribesmen while working on a task begin to chant "harambee;" this means together. Delegation leads to togetherness, and togetherness leads to effective task management. Dr. John Maxwell said, "Team work makes the dream work."

Investing time can also mean giving something time to yield result. If you want to invest in any portfolio, one of the questions you are asked is, how long you want to lock in the investment. If you break the stipulated time, you pay a steep penalty. When you invest, you have to wait or allow sufficient time for maturation. You do not plant a seed today and expect fruit a few seconds later. When you do not patiently wait, it leads to worry, and worry is nothing other than borrowed trouble. The worrying about tomorrow will empty the strength of today. God has been patient with you, also imbibe patience. He alone determines the time in any endeavor.

> Don't you realize how kind, tolerant, and patient God is with you? Or don't you care? Can't you see how kind he has been in giving you time to turn from your sin?
> (Romans 2: 4, NLT)

It is important to understand divine timetable for any event. The people of Issachar are described as understanding the times. It is a good thing to wait, but the wait cannot be endless. If it becomes prolonged, it leads to whining, which prevents winning. You need to understand when to act. Jesus Christ, when He was walking on a road, saw a fig tree, and He cursed the fig tree because it was just full of leaves and had no fruits. The Bible records that the fig tree should not have fruit at that time because it was not the season for fruit. Jesus Christ still cursed the tree. This means that there is a natural and spiritual season. If a man misses his spiritual season, he will never be able to operate in his natural season.

PROPHESY

Our spoken word is very important. It is directly related to the time we spend with or in the Word. The first word that came out of the mouth of the Most High was a prophecy "Let there be light." Subsequently, in Genesis chapter 1, we see God continuing to prophesy. This is one of the most important investments you can ever make.

> Then was brought unto Him one possessed with a devil, blind, and dumb: and He healed him, insomuch that the blind and dumb both spake and saw.
> (Matthew 12:22, KJV)

This story is intriguing because of its grammatical construction that emphasizes the importance of the ability to speak or prophesy. In English grammar, if you make an illustration using the word "respectively," it means there is an order of relative association. In the story, the sentence "the blind and dumb both spake and saw," will imply that blindness is associated with speaking and dumbness is associated with seeing. This is not what it should be. Blind and see are related while dumb and speak should be together. There was a divine reversal in the order to emphasize the importance of the spoken word (the word spake came first).

God already said that He honors His word above His name. To honor something means to respect, admire, and most importantly, to credit. If you speak the Word into your situation or circumstance, you are crediting your account. Something worthwhile is being remitted into your account, and you can appropriate what has been credited to you into whatever your need may be. You cannot be a babbler, but an aimer. Your word needs to be direct and accurate.

The psalmist said:

> Listen while I build my case, God, the most honest prayer you'll ever hear. Show the world I'm innocent—in your heart you know I am. Go ahead, examine me from inside out, surprise me in the middle of the night—You'll find I'm

just what I say I am. My words don't run loose.
(Psalm 17:1–3, MSG)

Your words must not run loose. There must be AIM—Attitude, Intensity, Momentum. As a king, we must speak with kingly attitude and kingly intensity so that there will be kingly momentum.

> God means what he says. What he says goes. His powerful Word is sharp as a surgeon's scalpel, cutting through everything, whether doubt or defense, laying us open to listen and obey. Nothing and no one is impervious to God's Word. We can't get away from it—no matter what.
> (Hebrews 4:12–13, MSG)

If God means what he says, we must also say what we mean. A man in need does not skirt or dance around issues. Most times because we do not understand and meditate on the Word of God, we start to babble. We need to be immersed in the Word so that we will be able to say what we mean. No one is impervious to God's Word. "We can't get away from it."

Listen to this carefully; "no one" means no one. God is not impervious to His own Word, and He also cannot get away from His Word. This should bring a smile to your face so that you can keep on saying His Word back to him. The effectual fervent prayer of the righteous accomplishes much (breaks down barriers).

> Then the LORD put forth his hand, and touched my mouth. And the LORD said unto me, Behold, I have put my words in thy mouth. (Jeremiah 1:9, KJV)

What he has put in our mouths is His words. Your voice can give melody to the word, but it must be His word.

The prophet that hath a dream, let him tell a dream; and he
that hath my word, let him speak my word faithfully. What
is the chaff to the wheat? saith the LORD.
(Jeremiah 23:28, KJV)

Anything other than His word looks like chaff. Invest in the
word of prophecy even if it does not look like it. Your today
could be bleak, but your tomorrow will be bright. We need to
call those things that be not as though they were.

By faith we understand that the worlds [during the suc-
cessive ages] were framed (fashioned, put in order, and
equipped for their intended purpose) by the Word of God,
so that what we see was not made out of things which are
visible. (Hebrews 11:3, TAB)

When you invest in prophesying, you are fashioning, putting in
order and equipping for its intended purpose. A man cannot be
said to be great if his children are vagabonds. The Word of God
says train a child... to train is an investment. While we can talk
about the material things we buy for our children, how about the
moral and spiritual upbringing?

Before they sleep at night, you read to them. A big question
is what do you read and say to them? Are you reading what will
give them nightmares, or what will challenge them to leave an
indelible positive print on the sand of time? Look at the pre-
mium that God places on investment.

For I have known (chosen, acknowledged) him [as My
own], so that he may teach and command his children and
the sons of his house after him to keep the way of the Lord
and to do what is just and righteous, so that the Lord may
bring Abraham what He has promised him.
(Genesis 18:19, TAB)

God said it is definite that Abraham will teach and command. When you teach or command, you talk and spend time. God is in effect saying that Abraham will be a great investor, and the effect was easily discernible in the life of Isaac. What cut short the Eden experience of Adam was his inability to invest in Eve.

> And the Lord God commanded the man, saying, You may freely eat of every tree of the garden; But of the tree of the knowledge of good and evil and blessing and calamity you shall not eat, for in the day that you eat of it you shall surely die. (Genesis 2:16–17, TAB)

The Lord commanded Adam, so he should have in turn commanded Eve so that there would be no ambiguity. Certain things do not warrant explanation. It is simply this is the way it should be. Sometimes our children ask questions, like "Why should I do this or that? In some cases we just have to let them know lovingly that it is because Daddy or Mummy says so. We try to democratize or liberalize everything to the peril of the home. When Satan came to Eve, her response showed that she wasn't sure of what Adam had told her.

> Now the serpent was more subtle and crafty than any living creature of the field which the Lord God had made. And he [Satan] said to the woman, Can it really be that God has said, You shall not eat from every tree of the garden? And the woman said to the serpent, We may eat the fruit from the trees of the garden, Except the fruit from the tree which is in the middle of the garden. God has said, You shall not eat of it, neither shall you touch it, lest you die.
> (Genesis 3: 1–3, TAB)

Hello! God did not say he commanded. A careful study of the word of God will reveal that there is a difference between the saying and the commanding of God.

Let all the earth fear the Lord [revere and worship Him]; let all the inhabitants of the world stand in awe of Him. For He spoke, and it was done; He commanded, and it stood fast. (Psalm 33: 8–9, TAB)

Let us look at the words "spoke" and "command" in terms of civilian and military personnel. We can liken the word "spoke" to the civilian side of God (gentle) and the word "command" to his military side (strict disciplinarian). A civilian can say something and you may flout it without too much retribution, but flout the command of a military officer, and the consequence could be severe. The speed with which a subordinate hastens to carry out the command of a superior officer is with immediate effect and automatic alacrity.

When God commands, it stands fast. It is immovable and unshakable. Investing in terms of the precise Word of God that we speak into our situations, circumstances and families is very important to be great. This is one of the reasons the psalmist said *"You'll find I'm just what I say I am. My words don't run loose"* (Psalm 17:3, MSG).

Let your words come undiluted no matter the situation staring you in the face, and you would have built the first pillar of greatness.

David said to Goliath that God will deliver Goliath into his hand; he will smite and take his head from him. This eventually came to pass. He called those things that be not as though they were.

INTELLECT

Our temperaments—sanguine, choleric, melancholic and phlegmatic—may differ, but however you look at your self, you are not worthless. Some can give ideas but cannot execute, while others will initiate the idea, polish it, and execute it. You are a special you. You have what others do not have. God did not make a mistake in creating you. That which you think is rubbish just needs refining so that the rare gem can glow.

Do not allow your esteem to be pummeled and played like ping-pong. You are not a factor to be manipulated on the assembly line of production. You are not a mistake.

William Arthur Ward said "Flatter me and I may not believe you. Criticize me and I may not like you. Ignore me and I may not forgive you. Encourage me and I will not forget you." All you need is encouragement, and that is what you are getting by reading this book. You are a special you; there are no two people like you. You are loaded by the creator; do not allow yourself to be lambasted by the created. Take time to build yourself up and polish yourself.

> Study to show thyself approved unto God, a workman that needeth not to be ashamed, rightly dividing the word of truth. (2 Timothy 2: 15, KJV)

No matter your status now, do not look down on yourself. You are a good and perfect gift from God. There is a special deposit in you. Remember the outward bound competence requires inward bound consistence.

MONEY

However little that we have, we need to invest. One of the reasons why most wage earners find it hard to invest is that they are not practicing the concept of deduction from source. When your pay check goes into your bank account, you must instruct the bank to automatically transfer a specified amount to a portfolio of your choice. As Christians, we have to learn to be faithful in our tithe and our offering. It is also an investment.

Bring all the tithes into the storehouse so there will be enough food in my Temple. If you do," says the **LORD** Almighty, "I will open the windows of heaven for you. I will pour out a blessing so great you won't have enough room to take it in! Try it! Let me prove it to you!
(Malachi 3:10, **NLT**)

When you invest, you sacrifice the short-term pain for the long-term gain. It will involve the saddling of your donkey. Donkeys are things that want to prevent you from investing.

SADDLE YOUR DONKEY

Then God said, "Take your son, your only son, Isaac, whom you love, and go to the region of Moriah. Sacrifice him there as a burnt offering on one of the mountains I will tell you about." Early the next morning Abraham got up and saddled his donkey. He took with him two of his servants and his son Isaac. When he had cut enough wood for the burnt offering, he set out for the place God had told him about. On the third day Abraham looked up and saw the place in the distance. (Genesis 22: 2–4, **NIV**)

A saddle is mostly referred to as a padded leather seat. In other cases it implies that one is in control or dominant (i.e. to saddle a situation, or sit in the saddle). A donkey, on the other hand, is referred to as a beast of burden, an obstinate or stupid situation. It is a situation that will not go away unless something is done about it. To get to the next dimension in kingdom excellence, there is always a donkey that needs to be saddled. The next dimension in kingdom excellence is only a decision away.

The situation to the ordinary may look stupid, but it is a donkey that needs to be saddled. Failure to firmly control such a situation may ultimately make a mockery of your kingship. Saddling a donkey is the ability to take the dream from the dungeon and dragons so that you can wear the diadem. When the instruction to sacrifice Isaac was given to Abraham, God was in effect telling him to make an investment. The investment was not only Isaac as a person, but also to prove his trust in the Most High God. Without a doubt the situation was stubborn because if he did not do it, the thought would keep on trailing him for the rest of his life.

He had to saddle (i.e. put to rest the situation). He took God's option to invest. Stubborn situations are what make an individual exclaim that all these things are against him. Stubborn situations are specific to all individuals. King Solomon exclaimed that there is nothing new under the sun. While the situation may not be new, its effect on you will be new. This is why people say "a whole new experience."

The earlier you saddle your donkey, the better. In the process of saddling a donkey, only trusted people can assist you, and there is a limit to which even the trusted few can assist you. Abraham rose up early in the morning and went with only two of his numerous servants. At a point he told the two to wait for him. To saddle a donkey, you have to be prepared. Controlling a difficult situation requires preparation and persistence, diligence and discipline.

The tests that we face in life may be similar, but they are not identical. Often times they are custom-made or tailor-made for you. A peculiar situation about the tests of life is that nobody can go through it for you. It is a designer outfit with your name boldly engraved on it. In those situations, people around you cannot help you. A test or stubborn situation is meant to see how you handle challenges.

Therefore, prepare your minds for action; be self controlled; set your hope fully on the grace to be given you when Jesus Christ is revealed. (1 Peter 1:13, **NIV**)

A truth about all donkey situations is that they have been designed so that you will control them.

> But remember that the temptations that come into your life are no different from what others experience. And **God is faithful.** He will keep the temptation from becoming so strong that you can't stand up against it. When you are tempted, he will show you a way out so that you will not give in to it. (1 Corinthians 10:13, NLT)

From our text in Genesis chapter 22, God had been speaking to Abraham about how great he will be and how the families of the earth will be blessed through him. After 30 years of constant repetition that made Abraham and Sarah to roll on the ground with laughter, God finally gave him the expected seed. Ironically, the same God came back to him and said he should go and sacrifice the seed. In essence, God said with your own hand go and kill *our vision*. Isaac was a vision from God that was gifted to Abraham; he could not die an untimely death. Whatever the vision that you have that is of and from God cannot die in Jesus' name.

Also, the instructions from God to Abraham were not clear; "go to the region of Moriah" (not specific), "sacrifice him on one of the mountains," but Abraham on the third day saw the place in the distance. He saw the place on the third day, not the first or the second, after he had ample opportunity to control the donkey. As you begin to control the donkey, the vision becomes clearer. When God presents a test or donkey before his children, it is always to make sure that you love or reverence him.

> Don't lay a hand on that boy! Don't touch him! Now I know how fearlessly you fear God; you didn't hesitate to place your son, your dear son, on the altar for me.
> (Genesis 22:12, MSG)

THE D'S THAT MAKE A DONKEY

There are five D's in the story about sacrificing Isaac that Abraham had to contend with to be able to control the stubborn and physically stupid situation. These Ds are the readily available options to us when a donkey needs to be saddled. They are the seemingly easy way to take instead of investing in our future. They always seem to be the best and only way out. There is a way that seems right to a man. It is only when you take care of this situation that you can invest in your future.

DEBT

The first option that Abraham had was to tell God, "You are my Daddy and You should understand; concerning this Isaac, (the child of my old age). Lord I owe You one, let Isaac be." Debt always looks like a solution, but it is a temporary and tentacled reprieve. You may not pay now, but you will definitely pay with interest later.

If you do not give God what He is asking from you, you will not be able to get what you did not ask for from Him. It is those things that you did not ask for that will make you excel in life (Solomon gave a thousand burnt offerings, and he later asked God for understanding, but God gave him much more). If you do not trust in Him, how are you going to know that He is called Jehovah Jireh? Abraham owed the debt of fidelity earlier. He cut corners when Sarah presented an option to assist God in fulfilling His purpose.

> ...so she said to Abram, "The LORD has kept me from having children. Go, sleep with my maidservant; perhaps I can build a family through her." Abram agreed to what Sarai said. (Genesis 16:2, NIV)

When another opportunity came to pay God in full, he did not slack. He decided to invest Isaac. *"Give generously, for your gifts will return to you later"* (Ecclesiastes 11:1, NLT).

There was a time God simply told Lot through the angels to go to the mountains, but he thought he knew more than the manufacturer and opted for Zoar. He owed God the debt of complete obedience. *"But Lot said to them, 'No, my lords, please!'"* (Genesis 19:18, NIV). When you do not do what God asks you to do correctly and completely, it is like investing at the wrong season; you either lose your principal, or the investment may yield no dividend.

DECEPTION

Abraham had to saddle deception because he was used to doing that; for example, when he came across challenges in the case of Pharaoh (Genesis 12:10–20) and Abimelech (Genesis 20:1–17), he lied about Sarah. Abraham could easily have gone in search of Ishmael and substituted him for Isaac. His mindset would then be that at least both their names start with "I." If you cannot find Isaac, use Ishmael. The aim is for blood to touch the soil.

Abraham could also have coached Isaac and instructed him to run for his dear life. He could have just told God, "The boy that you gave me is very strong and agile." "Immediately he saw the wood and fire he ran away." "To your tent O Isaac."

> Where can I go from your Spirit? Where can I flee from your presence? If I go up to the heavens, you are there; if I make my bed in the depths, you are there. If I rise on the wings of the dawn, if I settle on the far side of the sea, even there your hand will guide me, your right hand will hold me fast. If I say, "Surely the darkness will hide me and the light become night around me," even the darkness will not be dark to you;

the night will shine like the day, for darkness is as light to you. (Psalm 139:7–12, NIV)

You cannot deceive God; neither can you run from Him. All you have to do is ask Jonah. He thought he could hide in Tarshish when he was sent on a divine errand to Nineveh. If you think Jonah is an Old Testament believer, and we are under grace, then ask Ananias and Sapphira. The reason why we find it easy to deceive is because of a lack of the spirit of God.

Many deceivers, who do not acknowledge Jesus Christ as coming in the flesh, have gone out into the world. Any such person is the deceiver and the antichrist. (2 John 1:7, NIV)

DELAY

Abraham did not delay. He arose early in the morning. He knew what delay had done to the vision that God gave him. *"This was Stephen's reply: "Brothers and honorable fathers, listen to me. Our glorious God appeared to our ancestor Abraham in Mesopotamia before he moved to Haran"* (Acts 7:2, NLT).

God did not first speak to Abraham in Haran, but in Mesopotamia; but he detoured to Haran and wasted some time there. There is a story of a young man that was witnessed to, but said tomorrow we will talk about it; but he did not live to see the next day. Have you been delaying to totally surrender to Christ? *"I will hurry, without lingering, to obey your commands"* (Psalm 119:60, NLT).

DISOBEDIENCE

When God spoke to Abraham, he gave him specific instructions. *"Then the LORD told Abram, "Leave your country, your relatives, and your father's house, and go to the land that I will show you"*

(Genesis 12:1, NLT). Abraham disobeyed; he went with Lot, a relative. The disobedience delayed the wonderful plan of God for his life. This time around, Abraham totally obeyed.

In what areas have you been disobeying? Let me help you out. Are you living with a man or a woman that you are not married to? It is time to make amends. You should quickly make your way to the registry or the church for proper pre-marital counseling and solemnization so that the situation could be corrected. When you disobey the Word of God, you are making a negative investment. If there is any situation that you need to correct quickly, do so. For whatsoever a man sows, he shall reap.

DIVISION

Division is simply double-vision. Double-vision brings about myopia—an inability to see clearly. This was what caused the birth of Ishmael. The opposite of division is vision. Vision comes with unity while division comes with discord.

Abraham arrested division to have a vision ("on the third day, Abraham saw the place afar off"). He was focused on the assignment that God gave him. Abraham had a firm trust in the ability of God as a great provider. Due to this, he was able to prophesy that God will provide for himself a lamb.

> The next day John saw Jesus coming toward him and said, "Look! There is the Lamb of God who takes away the sin of the world! (John 1:29, NIV)

"Your ancestor Abraham rejoiced as he looked forward to my coming. He saw it and was glad." (John 8:56, NLT) The vision that Abraham saw was none other than Jesus the Lamb. Are you ready to see Him in your life today? If you have not surrendered your life to Him, He desires to be the commander-in-chief of your

life. No matter who, what or where you run to, if you don't have Him, there will be no peace and purpose.

HOW TO INVEST

Joyfully: The force of joy unlocks the potential in the seed.
Selectively: We are a product of the choices that we make.
Sacrificially or daringly: The pain of today yields the gain of tomorrow (uncommon result). You use today to get tomorrow.
Bountifully: If you want what you've never had, do what you've never done.
Prayerfully: The enabler and protector of every Godly investment.

WHERE TO INVEST

The **LORD** appeared to Isaac and said, "Do not go down to Egypt; live in the land where I tell you to live.
(Genesis 26:2, **NIV**)

There is a divine entrance or leading in anything that you attempt to do. The phrase "that same land" can mean: the land of famine, hunger, poverty or strange land. Most importantly it means the land that God commanded Isaac to live in. Ask God before investing. He has promised to instruct you in the way you will go and to guide you with His eyes on you.

NUGGETS

1. Invest means to sow (time, effort, resources), and it involves some sacrifice.
2. The principle of investing is intertwined with the law of seed and harvest based on the Word of God. This state that "while the earth remains, seed time, harvest shall not cease."
3. What to invest:
   - Time—focus on the vital issues that will promote, and propel you to your destiny.
   - Intellect—polish yourself up through the study of the Word.
   - Prophecy—speak the Word of God, and you will prophesy into your future. Remember that God honors His Word above His name.
   - AIM–Attitude, Intensity, Momentum.
   - Money—be faithful with your tithes and offerings. It is a commandment from God.
4. How to invest:
   - Joyfully
   - Selectively
   - Sacrificially
   - Bountifully
   - Prayerfully
5. Where to invest:
   - Invest in the things that the Lord has commanded you to.

PRAYER POINTS

- My God, help me to recognize what to sow, and give me the grace to sow; in Jesus' name.
- My Father, let what I sow bring forth abundantly. You have promised to multiply the seed I sow. Multiply my seeds, in Jesus' name.
- My King, let my harvest cover famine, hunger, poverty, nakedness or sorrow that may want to come my way.
- O Lord, let my investment turn me into an amazement, in Jesus' precious name.
- My Lord, give me the wisdom to invest my time wisely so I do not waste my life.
- I speak into my situation; there shall be a lifting up. I will be the head and not the tail. It shall be well with me in Jesus' name.
- Father, I choose to saddle my donkey and do what I need to do to achieve greatness. Oh Lord, elevate me to the next dimension of greatness.
- My God, prepare me for greatness; the persistence, preparation, diligence and discipline that I need, give unto me, in Jesus' name.
- My God and my King, remove every distraction from my life, every debt, deceit, delay, disobedience and division. Keep my focus on you, in Jesus' name.
- Lord, help me to invest joyfully, selectively, sacrificially, bountifully and prayerfully. Lead me to where I should invest.

INCREASE

They know enough who know how to learn.

-Henry Brooks Adams

"And the man waxed great." (Genesis 26:13, KJV)

The second pillar of greatness that we will be looking at is Increase. Isaac invested when he was not expecting much, but he got more than he bargained for. This will result in lots of challenges to overcome. Some of the challenges that stared Isaac in the face when he invested and made a profit were:

Where do I store the produce?
How soon can I build a silo?
What should be the dimension of the silo?
How do I prevent pests from destroying the crops?
How do I ward off marauders?
Was it a fluke?
Can I repeat it?
How and when do I buy more land?
What other crops do I plant?
What other farming methods should I use?
How many yoke of oxen do I buy?
How many oxen do I buy?
How many workers should I employ?
Who will be the farm manager?
Which countries do I export to?

For how much do I sell the crops?

Which crops should I produce the most?

Should I sell wholesale or open retail outlets?

How do I prevent this profit from coming between God and me?

How do I prevent this profit from disrupting my family?

These were some of the thoughts and huge decisions that Isaac had to contend with and make. Most of them had timelines and deadlines, but in all these challenges, the man waxed great. Isaac increased. What did he increase?

Taking a cue from Isaac, we are beset with such questions, situations, challenges and circumstances every day. What job should I do? Which profession should I pursue? Who should I marry? How many children should I have? In what area of the city should I live? Which church should I go to? The difference between the mediocre and the great ones is that the great ones made the right choices.

You only make the right choice from a position of strength, and strength is gained over time by exercise (either brain or brawn). You need to always put yourself in the position to make the right choice. Life is like a journey; there are always alternative routes to get to a location.

Life does not always give you what you deserve but what you decide. Do not make a decision when weary, worrying or hungry. If you feel pressured to make a decision, call time out. Two men going to the same place will likely get there at different times if they are not in the same car and if they take different routes. We are a product of the choice that we make. Greatness will not fall on your lap, but you must prepare and position yourself to do what is right. When preparation meets opportunity, testimony will follow.

For a student in an examination hall faced with multiple-choice questions, if the student has not studied, all the options will either look wrong or right. This student has not increased his odds of selecting the right answer because he failed to study. Another student that has taken the pain to burn the proverbial midnight oil will do what is called elimination by substitution. The latter student will be making choices based on knowledge.

Looking at the first pillar of greatness, which is investing, a principal reason why we invest is because we desire an increase. We must invest in the right thing to get any increase. A good grasp of the word "wax" will help in understanding the concept of increase as it relates to pillars of greatness. To wax great implies a progressive increase. Wax as a noun refers to a substance that is used as a protection or shield. Wax is solid at normal temperature and liquid when heated. This allows it to flow and also take the shape of the environment. The fluidity of the wax represents flexibility and adaptability. Isaac was flexible enough to listen to fresh ideas and learn new concepts. He was also fluid enough to adapt to the vagaries of his new found wealth.

Isaac would not have waxed great if he did not increase the odds of making a success of his sudden wealth. Taking the wrong turn would have led to a dead end, or a downward spiral. He had to increase his ability to do what is right. Any dough that hates the challenge of the heat from an oven will never rise, and consequently the dough will never become a choice pastry. Do you know what keeps the dough going is a focus on what it wants to become? The heat, though working together with the dough to produce a delicacy, can also be looked at as a discomfort, but the dough will withstand the challenge.

In the same vein, despite all the weight that so easily beset us right left and center, we need to increase our focus to get to our destined location. This leads us to the first thing that we need to increase.

FOCUS

With all the myriad of questions going on in the mind of Isaac because of the sudden profit, he had to do the right things. He had to be able to overcome the challenges he was encountering. A man that loses focus will never arrive at a destination. He is like those that Apostle James described as being tossed to and fro. He or she is double-minded. Focus implies that in a journey from point A to point Z, the Bs, Cs and Ys encountered are necessary transit points, but they are not the ultimate end. When you look at transit, it means if focus is lost, you can get down at the wrong stop. It is from the word "transit" that we get "transition," which means evolution, change over, make-over, alteration, shift, move, modification or conversion.

Many have been converted or transitioned to what God did not purpose for them. Some Christians from a Christian home have been converted to what God did not intend them to be. Some have embraced wrong doctrines in a quest for an identity that was not lost. *"For in Him we live, and move, and have our being;"* (Acts 17:28, KJV). If you are not in Him, without a doubt you will be out of Him. If you are out of Him, you are out of His will, and if you are out of His will, you are out in the cold on your own—"For outside are the dogs."

Every day we go through and also see lots of distractions, but we must increase our focus on the objective. What are you trying to achieve in life? The lofty heights attained by few were only reached by being focused. Focus implies concentration. This does not mean that there will not be distractions or distracting elements, but it simply means you are not discouraged or sidetracked. The word "concentration" can also mean absorption or meditation. Meditate on the objective and the purpose when you find yourself wanting to lose your objective. Sing it to yourself. Shout it to yourself. Turn it to a testimony.

And Isaac went out to meditate in the field at the eventide: and he lifted up his eyes, and saw, and, behold, the camels were coming. (Genesis 24:63, KJV)

While Eliezer (Abraham's servant) was on his way from looking for a wife for Isaac, Isaac was meditating, pondering, reflecting, thinking of what he wants in a wife, what his wife will look like, when his wife will show up. While he was still meditating, his wife showed up. A deep concentration or meditation has a way of bringing to reality what we have pictorially drawn up in our minds.

> This book of the law shall not depart out of thy mouth; but thou shalt meditate therein day and night, that thou mayest observe to do according to all that is written therein: for then thou shalt make thy way prosperous, and then thou shalt have good success. (Joshua 1:8, KJV)

Every individual, especially a child of God, has the ability to make his way prosperous. To those that believe, he gives power to be called the children of God. Hold tenaciously unto what you believe in. The mere fact that what you believe in is beginning to take shape does not mean you should lose your focus. A farmer that puts a seed in the soil and now sees the seed sprouting does not stop caring for the seedling. The farmer has to water, weed, fertilize and protect against insects and rodents. Albeit there is a sense of joy when the seed sprouts, but it is not where the farmer wants to be. He wants to see the seed mature to either a food or cash crop, depending on what has been planted.

It is very easy to lose focus when there is a false sense of success. Focus is the ability to define the objective, not the problem or the temporary relief. For the Judo, karate or tae-kwon-do fighters who break bricks with parts of their body, the simple concept they use to be a success is by defining the objective. Their objective is not really to break the brick, but to get past the brick. The brick is the problem. The fighter simply focuses on the object below the brick. Many people fall short in their quest to get to their destination because they focus on the problem.

When you know where you are going and your mind is settled that this is where you want to be, then it becomes easy to stay on course. There has to be an inner resolve to be above and not beneath. Situations are always there for you to overcome. This is the reason why we have the noun "overcomer" (i.e. those that encountered difficulties and towered above them).

In a baseball game there is a pitcher, and some of the pitches in his arsenal are fastballs, change-ups and curveballs. You also have hitters that takes a stance, dig in and before you know it they not only have a hit but a home run. The pitcher may have thrown two strikes, but until the third strike is thrown, the hitter is still at the home plate ready to hit. The hitter never looses the focus to connect with the ball. Do not lose your focus. Life may have thrown you a fastball, a change up, a curveball or a slider, but you are about to connect and hit a grand slam. The only condition is to keep the focus.

THE POWER OF FOCUS

Then after a time his master's wife cast her eyes upon Joseph, and she said, Lie with me. But he refused and said to his master's wife, See here, with me in the house my master has concern about nothing; he has put all that he has in my care. He is not greater in this house than I am; nor has he kept anything from me except you, for you are his wife. How then can I do this great evil and sin against God? She spoke to Joseph day after day, but he did not listen to her, to lie with her or to be with her Then it happened about this time that Joseph went into the house to attend to his duties, and none of the men of the house were indoors. And she caught him by his garment, saying, Lie with me! But he left his garment in her hand and fled and got out [of the house] (Genesis 39:7–12, **TAB**)

Above is an excerpt from the story of a young boy named Joseph who was sold into slavery by his brothers because he had a dream. Despite the persecution, Joseph held onto his dream. He did not allow his focus to sway. The master's wife wanted to abort his dream. She would have accomplished this if Joseph gave in to her demand, but Joseph refused. He not only refused, but he also recounted his experience in the master's house; how good the master has been to him. Joseph was encouraging himself with all the things he was saying and at the same time increasing his focus. He was keeping his eyes on the dream. For all those that are reading this book or browsing, no matter what you are going through, inasmuch as you are still alive, there is still hope. The Word of God says a living dog is better than a dead lion. You may be eating crumbs at the moment, but the choice delicacy is not far away. I remember a story from my daddy in the Lord, the General Overseer of The Redeemed Christian Church of God, Pastor E.A. Adeboye. He recounted the early years of his marriage when he and his wife used to share the kind of meat called raincoat (hide). This was one of the cheapest meats, and the nutritional value is also very low. He said he used to tell his wife, "Our tomorrow will be alright." Then they ate hide; today they can eat caviar if they so desire.

> If a tree is cut down, there is hope that it will sprout again
> and grow new branches. Though its roots have grown old in
> the earth and its stump decays at the scent of water it may
> bud and sprout again like a new seedling.
> (Job 14:7–9, NLT)

While the master's wife cast her eyes on Joseph, Joseph cast his eyes on God. Who or what are you looking at?

> Therefore, since we are surrounded by such a huge crowd of
> witnesses to the life of faith, let us strip off every weight that
> slows us down, especially the sin that so easily hinders our

progress. And let us run with endurance the race that God has set before us. We do this by keeping our eyes on Jesus, on whom our faith depends from start to finish. (Hebrew 12:1–2, NLT)

I will lift up mine eyes unto the hills, from whence cometh my help. My help cometh from the LORD, *which made heaven and earth.* (Psalm 121:1–2, KJV) "I will" is present continuous. It is a conscious act, an effort. It is not about doing it today and forgetting to do it tomorrow. Even if it seems as if I cannot see success and shadows and gloom surround me, yet I will. Keep focusing. Increase your focus despite all distractions. Brother Habakkuk said:

Though the fig tree may not blossom, Nor fruit be on the vines; Though the labor of the olive may fail, And the fields yield no food; Though the flock may be cut off from the fold, And there be no herd in the stalls—Yet I will rejoice in the LORD, I will joy in the God of my salvation. (Habakkuk 3:17–18, NKJV)

One can quickly surmise that this prophet was going through challenging times. Fig trees were not blossoming, no fruit on the vines—this means there were no cash crops and nothing to sell or export. The field was yielding no food—this implies that there were no food crops. To compound this difficult period, there were no flock or herd. We can virtually say there was nothing for this man, but in all these, Habakkuk said he will rejoice. Why was he able to rejoice? Because he had a focus. Let us look back at a statement that Habakkuk made:

Then the LORD answered me and said: "Write the vision and make it plain on tablets, That he may run who reads it. For the vision is yet for an appointed time; But at the end it

will speak, and it will not lie. Though it tarries, wait for it; Because it will surely come, It will not tarry.
(Habakkuk 2:2–3, NKJV)

From the two verses above, you can see why Habakkuk, despite the challenges, could rejoice. He knew what God had shown him, he wrote it down, and he also realized that God is not a man that he should lie. What God had promised, he would accomplish. Habakkuk was able to focus on what God had said, not the distractions or light afflictions that are but for a moment.

Going back to Joseph and the master's wife, this woman told him to lie with her. To lie means to bend down, stoop low, prostrate or to lay horizontally. Joseph knew that to lie with her would mean denigrating himself. God did not say to lie down; God said "arise and shine for your light is come and the glory of the Lord is risen upon you."

A shift in focus from God will spell the end of any dream that you may have. Joseph was able to refuse her advances because his focus remained one and the same.

The light of the body is the eye: if therefore thine eye be single, thy whole body shall be full of light.
(Matthew 6: 22, KJV)

Joseph recognized that anything that he did wrong would be against the King of kings. "She spoke to Joseph day after day." Listen carefully; everyday you are faced with challenges against your dream and vision, but keep your focus. Increase your focus.

DILIGENCE

This word means to be industrious, meticulous, thorough, attentive to detail. Diligence must be increased. With Isaac's new fortune, it was very easy to be sloppy or slothful, but the Word of God says the man waxed great. If he became sloppy, it could have been, "The man tumbled like a pack of cards."

There is the story of a man regarded as the madman in the territory of the Gadarenes (Mark 5:1–15). His story portrays diligence in madness. This man's madness could be classified as grade A madness. In the hierarchy of madmen, he could be regarded as chairman. While other madmen were in mental institutions, he could not be arrested; he was staying in a tomb. As much as people tried to chain him, they could not. He could not be restricted nor confined. At night, he was atop the mountain while others were sleeping, and during the daytime he would be in the tombs. *Confirmation from God! Aug 30th 2022*

When you look at the significance of going to the mountain, it means to go and recharge your spiritual battery. You go to the mountain to pray and seek the face of the Lord. As he diligently went to the mountain ("*And always, night and day, he was in the mountains*" Mark 5:5, KJV), Jesus Christ noticed him because the Word of God says through Jesus, "*Let us pass over unto the other side*" (Mark 4:35, KJV). Jesus Christ saw his diligence and decided to help him out by relieving him of his mental dysfunction. Others may not notice your diligent act, but God can see it. You have to be detail-oriented. Diligence breeds excellence. You must not be indolent.

POSITIVE HABITS: ROUTINE, LIFESTYLE BEHAVIOR

But when Daniel learned that the law had been signed, he went home and knelt down as usual in his upstairs room, with its windows open toward Jerusalem. He prayed three times a day, just as he had always done, giving thanks to his God. (Daniel 6:10, NLT)

What you repeatedly do, you will eventually reflect. Positive habit is very important in achieving success. Success is by conscious design, not accident. Routine can be monotonous, but its effect can be momentous. Nobody has ever achieved success without positive habits. There was a man called blind by the gate of a temple called beautiful. Every day he was placed by this gate, and he never complained. He was faithful to do his duty, which was to beg. On a destined day, Peter and John were going into the temple and they met this man, and his circumstances changed. He came to the gate blind, but he left the gate rejoicing. Many people have been absent from their duty post on their day of destiny.

DETERMINATION

Determination is a resolve, strength of mind, will power or commitment to achieve a goal. When you are committed to an objective, it shows your desire to conquer. When Job was going through a turbulent time in his life; everything he did demonstrated a resolve to be a winner. His wife came with a wonderful idea for her to become a widow. She said, "curse God and die." This would have been an open door for her to remarry if the husband is dead, but Job displayed strength of mind by refusing her counsel. Job maintained his integrity. Later on Job had to let everybody know where he stood when he said, *"Because even if he killed me, I'd keep on hoping"* (Job 13:15, MSG).

Though he slay me, yet will I trust in him.
(Job 13:15, KJV)

Determination is the difference between reaching your destination and making a shipwreck of your destiny. It is fueled by a vision of the possibilities of God, not the impossibilities of circumstances.

When the Philistines heard that David had been anointed king over all Israel, they mobilized all their forces to capture him. But David was told they were coming, so he and his men marched out to meet them. The Philistines had arrived in the valley of Rephaim and raided it. So David asked God, "Should I go out to fight the Philistines? Will you hand them over to me?" The LORD replied, "Yes, go ahead. I will give you the victory." So David and his troops went to Baal-perazim and defeated the Philistines there. "God has done it!" David exclaimed. "He used me to burst through my enemies like a raging flood!" So that place was named Baal-perazim (which means "the Lord who bursts through").
(1 Chronicles 14:8–11, NLT)

David and his men marched out to meet the Philistines. This was an action that portrayed determination. When you encounter situations that are contrary or that make it impossible humanly for you to reach your goal, the flesh will speak in an echo, "Give up! Give up..." but the spirit of God in you will be ringing alarm bells that you should "Press on..." You will make a choice based on what controls you. If you are led by the spirit of God and your focus is not on what you see, which are temporal, it will be easy for you to submit to the gentle nudge to press on. Determination is not about who or what you are facing, but it is all about the one you are serving. The Word of God said David and his men marched out to meet the philistines. This was easy because David had been used to marching out. When he confronted Goliath, he ran towards Goliath because he knew who he was committed to.

When a man gets serious about his God-given vision, Satan gets serious about him. Immediately David was anointed king over all Israel. Satan organized the philistines against him. Satan is always aiming to challenge your kingship. He does this by sowing a seed of doubt in your mind or by mysteriously afflict-

widely uses T.V programing.

ing you. When there is a blessed assurance concerning any decision you have made, hold on. Have you ever wondered why it is
only when you seem to be making headway that Satan will try
to throw a wrench in your wheel? Satan is not interested in failures because he understands that they are going nowhere. It was
when the daughter of Jairus was 12 years old that death struck.
Death did not strike at five months or five years. At 12 years, the
girl started making some intelligent decisions that Satan could
not ignore. If you are going through challenges, be more resolute
there is sunshine after rain. *Enemy's tool - make you not know who you are.*
When a man does not understand his design, he does not
know his destination and therefore he cannot be distinct. Let the
same man have a lofty dream the next thing could be a dungeon.
You have to know what you are committed to. If you must reach
your goal, there must be selective abandonment. Distinguish between the merely important and the massively important. You
have to get your priorities right.

> He was in the world, the world was there through Him,
> and yet the world didn't even notice. He came to His own
> people, but they didn't want Him. But whoever did want
> Him, who believed He was who He claimed and would do
> what He said, He made to be their true selves, their child-
> of-God selves. (John 1:10–12, MSG)

Whoever did want Him? Do you want Him? Is it apparent to
everybody that you want Him? Do you believe He is who He
claims and would do what He said? In another vein, do you really want what you are clamoring for, or it is just pretense? Know
the one you trust, and hold on to him.

> And God chose me to be a preacher, an apostle, and a teach-
> er of this Good News. And that is why I am suffering here
> in prison. But I am not ashamed of it, for I know the one in

whom I trust, and I am sure that he is able to guard what I
have entrusted to him until the day of his return.
(2 Timothy 1:11–12, NLT)

A decision to be determined is always met by resistance.

And as we tarried there many days, there came down from
Judaea a certain prophet, named Agabus. And when he was
come unto us, he took Paul's girdle, and bound his own
hands and feet, and said, Thus saith the Holy Ghost, So
shall the Jews at Jerusalem bind the man that owneth this
girdle, and shall deliver him into the hands of the Gentiles.
(Acts 21:10–11, KJV)

Depression is a tool used to get us out our purpose.

A battle that every individual must fight and win is that of the
mind. When a part of the mind is saying, "This decision, though
difficult, is the best course of action," another part will be pointing out all the difficulties attached to that decision. Before you
can win outside, you have to first win inside. Many kingdoms,
nations and kings that fell not only in the Bible but in history
first fell morally before falling militarily. Paul was faced with a
decision to make, and he was even presented with reasons not
to make the right decision, but because he had already won the
battle of the mind, he was able to win when human counsel
came.

Determination is the difference between who you are and
what you are.

And he left the oxen, and ran after Elijah, and said, Let me,
I pray thee, kiss my father and my mother, and then I will
follow thee. And he said unto him, Go back again: for what
have I done to thee? (1 Kings 19:20, KJV)

"Who" you are reflects the flesh. Ralph Waldo Emerson said
"Who you are speaks so loudly that I cannot hear what you say."

When who you are begins to speak, it robs you of the drive and determination that you need to do anything of significance. Who you are will always remind you of your position or status. Who you are will tell you that you are too big for that task and that the individual that gave the assignment is beneath you, whatever that means. Such people cannot do anything worthwhile unless a title is attached to what they are doing. Elisha was plowing with a yoke of oxen when Elijah's cloak was thrown upon him. He could have said, "What an insult!" But he understood the significance of that action. He willingly complied. If "who you are" is not put aside, you will not be able to download what the heavens are speaking.

Determined action(s) are foolishness to the wise.

> And the **LORD** spake unto Moses face to face, as a man speaketh unto his friend. And he turned again into the camp: but his servant Joshua, the son of Nun, a young man, departed not out of the tabernacle. (Exodus 33:11, KJV)

If you cannot serve, you cannot lead, which also means that you cannot be great. I have heard the testimonies of many people that are called great today, and one thing always stand out—their determination to serve. A pastor once shared how his colleagues used to ridicule him when he was serving the pastor before him. People said he was sucking up. Today, history can tell who is sucking up. When Joshua was always taking care of Moses, people would have mocked him. When he was eventually selected as the next leader of Israel, the people that berated him would eventually bow down for him. Whatever you are doing right now, that is "right service" without ulterior motive. Please continue to do it. You are sowing a seed, and the Bible says you will not plant and another harvest, you will not build and another inhabit. Your labor is not in vain. Do not depart from the tabernacle of triumph.

Determination is the pathway to the throne.

And the LORD said unto Moses, Come up to me into the
mount, and be there: and I will give thee tables of stone, and
a law, and commandments which I have written; that thou
mayest teach them. And Moses rose up, and his minister
Joshua: and Moses went up into the mount of God.
(Exodus 24:12–13,KJV)

Joshua is referred to as the minister of Moses. A minister is one
who is faithful. When you are close to the one you are serving,
you see the faults that others do not see. What you decide to do
with the faults will determine whether you will get to the throne
or not. The flesh could be screaming to you that you are more
eloquent to the hearing of the people, acceptable in the sight of
the people, educated in the estimate of the people and anointed
in your own mind. Disregard what the flesh has to say. It is the
spirit that quickens, and the flesh profits nothing. When Moses
was asked to come to the mount, Joshua did not complain that
he was tired; neither did he question why they had to climb
the mount again. He simply followed. Immediately Moses rose
up, Joshua did the same. Every sacrifice that Joshua made was
noticed by God. He later sat on the throne vacated by Moses at
his demise.

Determination brings conquest.

And Abraham rose up early in the morning, and saddled
his ass, and took two of his young men with him, and Isaac
his son, and clave the wood for the burnt offering, and rose
up, and went unto the place of which God had told him.
(Genesis 22:3, KJV)

Growth & Comfort don't go together

Whatever you are unwilling to confront, you will never conquer.
The instruction given to Abraham here was not what he would
love to hear, but he still obeyed. It takes determination to obey

instructions that will give victory. The movie *Rocky* is without a doubt the story of determination. It takes a determined man to wake up while every body is sleeping to run miles upon miles. It also takes determination to go into the ring and slug it out with a man that is bigger than you in size. Sometimes you enter into your office and look at the tasks set before you, and you can either systematically delve into it or quit. For those that venture, you are always surprised at the end of the day how much ground you have covered.

HOW TO COPE WITH CHALLENGES TO OUR DETERMINED ACTIONS

Give the devil no option

> Shadrach, Meshach, and Abednego answered the king, O Nebuchadnezzar, it is not necessary for us to answer you on this point. If our God Whom we serve is able to deliver us from the burning fiery furnace, He will deliver us out of your hand, O king. But if not, let it be known to you, O king, that we will not serve your gods or worship the golden image which you have set up! (Daniel 3:16–18, TAB)

When Daniel, Shadrach, Mesach and Abednego were thrown into the lion's den, and the fiery furnace, they were determined to stand up for God. They did not give the devil any option. There was no negotiation or bargaining. They simply told the king that the Lord they serve is able to save them. Even if He does not, He will still be God.

The alternative that the devil would have presented to them from the mouth of the king already came from them. Lots of times when we are about to take a step that requires strong determination, the devil will whisper "What if..." By listening to "what if," we would have abandoned the action that could move us towards our God-ordained destiny. Stop listening to the careless whispers of the devil, and be determined.

The people of Babylon tried to cover the glory of the Lord by changing the names of the Hebrew children:

Shadrach–Command of Aku
Mesach–Who is as Aku
Abednego–Servant of Nebo

The word "Aku" means moon god, and "Nebo" means god of science and literature. Compare the meaning of these names to their Hebrew names:

Hananiah–Gift of the Lord
Mishael–Who is what God is
Azariah–Whom Jehovah helps

When they found themselves in the fiery furnace, a combination of their original Hebrew names made a way for them. God proved to be who he is by providing help through a precious gift, his only begotten son. The king testified that three people were sent into the fiery furnace, but he can now see four people. The form of the fourth looked like that of the son of God. Jehovah the ever present help came to their rescue. Whatever you are facing, the ever present help will come through for you right early in Jesus' name. Do not negotiate with Satan. Give him no option.

ENTERTAIN NO UNNECESSARY CONVERSATION

Yes I know, keep your peace. (2 Kings 2:3, KJV)

When Elisha was following his master Elijah, the sons of the prophets were hounding him, making fun of him but Elisha did not go into any unnecessary conversation with them. He simply said politely, "shut up." I once heard a saying that said do not go into battle with a fool because when he has taken you to his level, he will then beat you with experience. Silence cannot be misquoted.

DO WHAT YOU HAVE BEEN DOING.

> Now when Daniel knew that the writing was signed, he went into his house, and his windows being open in his chamber toward Jerusalem, he got down upon his knees three times a day and prayed and gave thanks before his God, as he had done previously. (Daniel 6:10, TAB)

Daniel prayed as he had always done when a decree was signed to cause his downfall. He did not allow himself to be intimidated; he not only prayed but he also opened the window so that everybody will know on whose side he was. Do not stop your right actions; it will give the right answer.

BE STRONG

Determination is a will power that comes from within. Joshua, when he became leader, was advised by God and the Israelites to be strong. Those that know their God shall be strong, and they shall do exploits. The fuel for strength is the knowledge of God. God has never abandoned his children, and he is not a failure.

why we must constantly READ & spend time ɔ God.

> In conclusion, be strong in the Lord [be empowered through your union with Him]; draw your strength from Him [that strength which His boundless might provides].
> (Ephesians 6:10, TAB)

NUGGETS

- Life is about making the right choices/decisions, and it is full of challenges that must be overcome.
- Greatness is not something that is thrust upon you, but it is something one must achieve through dedication.
- You must make the right investment if you desire an increase.
- In order to attain an increase in the investment one must be:
- Focused—concentrate on the objective and not on the problem.
- Diligent—be industrious, thorough and meticulous. Diligence breeds excellence.
- Positive—your routine or behavior must be progressive.
- Determined—you must have the resolve, strength of mind or will power to increase.
- Wise—you must exercise good judgement.
- Discerning—you must be able to detect right from wrong.
- Protective—you must guard your heart diligently.

PRAYER POINTS

- My God, let me make right choices from a position of strength in Jesus' victorious name.
- My God, prepare and position me to do what is right to attain greatness.
- My Savior, increase me progressively.
- Lord, I want to be focused on you and on your vision for my life; increase my focus, in Jesus' mighty name.
- Lord, the diligence that breeds excellence, give unto me in Jesus' name, Amen.
- My King, I am determined to reach the top; help me to get there.
- The strength and will that takes one to the throne, Lord, give unto me.
- My God, make me overcome every opposition against your plans and vision for my life.
- My Lord, make me discerning, to know right from wrong and also take the right course of action.
- Oh God, through grace, make me industrious, thorough and meticulous so that I can achieve my God-given dream.

INITIATE

The people who get on in this world are the people who get up and look for the circumstances they want, and if they can't find them, make them.

- George Bernard Shaw

...and went forward (Genesis 26:13, KJV)

Looking at the life of Isaac, you see a man that wanted to be all that God had purposed him to be. Despite the fact that he reaped a bountiful yield on his investment and he increased in every sphere considerably, he was not satisfied with where he was. He had a deep and distinct desire to advance. He moved forward. The opposite of moving forward is to stagnate or be stagnant. One thing that any individual needs to do so as not to vegetate is to move forward. To move forward implies growth or enlargement. There are three members of the Trinity and they all abhor stagnancy. To be stagnant means to be sluggish, inert, inactive or dormant. Every time that God sees stagnancy, He moves in to correct the situation. *"Back at Horeb, God, our God, spoke to us: "You've stayed long enough at this mountain."*(Deuteronomy 1:6, MSG)

The Holy Spirit did the same thing. *"The earth was without form and an empty waste, and darkness was upon the face of the very great deep. The Spirit of God was moving (hovering, brooding) over the face of the waters."*(Genesis 1:2, TAB) The earth was once without movement, motionless, but the spirit of God

There are over also the signs of depression & loss of hope

moved or brooded. The word "brood" here means to sit on, or incubate like a hen on her eggs. This will ensure that the eggs are kept warm for the chicks to develop and subsequently hatch. The hen that provides warmth must be alive to generate heat. In other words, we can say stagnation means death while movement means life.

Jesus also did the same.

sadly this is how I feel about my parents home.

Now there is in Jerusalem a pool near the Sheep Gate. This pool in the Hebrew is called Bethesda, having five porches (alcoves, colonnades, doorways). In these lay a great number of sick folk—some blind, some crippled, and some paralyzed (shriveled up)—waiting for the bubbling up of the water. For an angel of the Lord went down at appointed seasons into the pool and moved and stirred up the water; whoever then first, after the stirring up of the water, stepped in was cured of whatever disease with which he was afflicted. There was a certain man there who had suffered with a deep-seated and lingering disorder for thirty-eight years. When Jesus noticed him lying there [helpless], knowing that he had already been a long time in that condition, He said to him, Do you want to become well? [Are you really in earnest about getting well?] The invalid answered, Sir, I have nobody when the water is moving to put me into the pool; but while I am trying to come [into it] myself, somebody else steps down ahead of me. Jesus said to him, Get up! Pick up your bed (sleeping pad) and walk! (John 5:2–8, TAB)

Above is the story of a man that was helpless and hopeless and his life was stagnant. When Jesus noticed him lying helpless, he stepped in to correct the situation despite the fact that the man appeared not ready to receive healing.

The heart desire of God for all his children is to progressively move forward. When a man begins to move forward, that man is displaying initiative, or initiating something. To initiate means to start or begin something, to introduce to a new field, interest, skill, or activity. One of the hardest steps in any endeavor or enterprise is the first, the baby steps. When a baby is attempting to walk, there will be a couple of falls but a baby still keeps on trying. Those that are not able to take the baby steps never take the adult step.

Initiative is the ability to either do what others have not done or to do what others have done better (i.e. to add value). When a man initiates, he is stirring up the gifts of God in him. Paul told Timothy:

> This is why I remind you to fan into flames the spiritual gift God gave you when I laid my hands on you. For God has not given us a spirit of fear and timidity, but of power, love, and self-discipline. (2 Timothy 1:6–7, NLT)

To everyone, God has given talents. No matter the lie that the devil wants you to believe, you are talented. You have a responsibility to use what God has given unto you. If you do not do anything about it, nobody will know you have it. As Paul told Timothy, fan into flames the talents of God in you. God has not given you the spirit of fear or timidity. Other translations of 2 Timothy Chapter 1: verse 6 says, *"stir up, keep ablaze, rekindle."* All this implies that you have the "giftings" (the continual working of the power of God in you). Giftings lead to liftings; you shall be lifted in Jesus' name. Amen.

No matter the lofty height that you have attained, the desire of God is for you to be a functioning being, not a vegetable nor a couch potato. A commitment to create and re-create will make sure you are in high demand. In this day, you see lots of companies setting aside a budget for training. This stems from the realization that there are always new and improved developments that will enhance the growth of the company. Since the human resource is the key in any enterprise, this resource must always be abreast of information that can help or accelerate the growth of the company.

Whenever you initiate anything, you must be guided by the "true north;" that is, will God be pleased with what I am about to start? I once heard a real life story of a young man, the son of a man of God that started an escort agency (mostly a glorified term for prostitution business) in his quest to be rich. The father refused to partake in the gains of this kind of business. You have to be careful that you are not birthing a strange fire.

> Aaron's sons Nadab and Abihu put coals of fire in their incense burners and sprinkled incense over it. In this way, they disobeyed the LORD by burning before him a different kind of fire than he had commanded. So fire blazed forth from the LORD's presence and burned them up, and they died there before the LORD. Then Moses said to Aaron, "This is what the LORD meant when he said, 'I will show myself holy among those who are near me. I will be glorified before all the people'." And Aaron was silent.
> (Leviticus 10:1–3, NLT)

When you birth strange fire, the Divine fire will definitely consume you and the strange fire. My prayer is that this will not be your portion, in Jesus' name.

WHAT YOU SHOULD NOT INITIATE

Because others are starting something does not mean you have to start something if God has not given you the leading. There should always be a divine entrance in everything that we do.

DO NOT INITIATE A LIE.

Satan is called the father of lies. Do not become a foster child of Satan because you want fame. *"So I killed him," the Amalekite* told David, *"for I knew he couldn't live. Then I took his crown and one of his bracelets so I could bring them to you, my lord."* (2 Samuel 1:*10*, NLT)

This man lied because he thought David would decorate him due to the death of the perceived enemy of David (Saul). He told the truth that Saul was dead, but he blatantly lied when he claimed he was the killer.

> Saul groaned to his armor bearer, "Take your sword and kill me before these pagan Philistines run me through and humiliate me." But his armor bearer was afraid and would not do it. So Saul took his own sword and fell on it.
> (1 Samuel 31:4, NLT)

One thing that is clear is that Saul killed himself. Be careful what you are starting.

DO NOT INITIATE CONFUSION.

> And David realized that the LORD had made him king over Israel and had made his kingdom great for the sake of his people Israel. After moving from Hebron to Jerusalem, David married more wives and concubines, and he had many sons and daughters. (2 Samuel 5:12–13, NLT)

This action of David resulted in confusion and disorder in his household. The children of David were not united. A house divided against itself cannot stand. ➔ My family / parents

God is a God of order, not confusion. The divine plan of God for man is one Eve to an Adam and one Adam to an Eve. It is also not Adam and Andrew, neither is it Eve and Evelyn. The hallmark of success is not concubines. What represents your own concubine? Is it food, pride, lust, covetousness? Concubines cause confusion and confusion leads to calamity.

another tool the enemy uses.

If you are the type that wants to attain greatness at all costs, not caring whose ox is gored, watch out. Attaining greatness at all costs could involve doing heinous things in order to get into the good books of your superior at your place of work. This shows you have no scruples. God will not be pleased, and there will definitely be consequences.

> Tampering with evidence—the Master does not approve of such things. (Lamentations 3:36, MSG),

> To deprive a man of justice- would not the Lord see such things? (Lamentations 3:36, NIV),

> To subvert a man in his cause, the LORD approveth not (Lamentations 3:36, KJV)

Remember, righteousness exalts, but sin is a reproach.

WHAT YOU SHOULD INITIATE

Honesty

The hallmark of any great endeavour or individual is what it is founded on. People appreciate openness. He that comes to equity must come with clean hands. When a man or woman says something, one thing everybody wants to be sure about is its sincerity, truthfulness, integrity, candour.

> And we, who with unveiled faces all reflect the Lord's glory, are being transformed into his likeness with ever-increasing glory, which comes from the Lord, who is the Spirit.
> (2 Corinthians 3:18, NIV)

Must walk & live in TRUTH!

To reflect the glory of God, you need an unveiled face. A face that can be discerned; someone whose yes is yes and no is no.

God is always looking for honesty in individuals. This is an attribute that separated David from Saul. David will always own up
despite his errors. Moses told the truth that he stammers, Jacob
told the truth that he was a usurper when he was asked his name
and God changed it to Israel.

> And all of us have had that veil removed so that we can be
> mirrors that brightly reflect the glory of the Lord.
> (2 Corinthians 3:18, NLT)

If the veil is not removed, you cannot brightly reflect the glory of
the Lord. A mirror that is not properly cleaned will present a distorted image. You cannot misrepresent yourself on your resume
while looking for a job. It does not matter if your friends tell you
to add an experience that you do not have on your resume, do
not do it. The question you need to ask yourself is if others that
know you intimately see this resume, how will they view you?
Most importantly, will God be happy with this? The chairman
of Merrill Lynch, John Tully, will call brokers when they make a
large profit of millions of dollars to ask them a simple question:
"If the New York Times put how you did it on the front page,
will you be proud."

> As God's messenger, I give each of you this warning: Be hon-
> est in your estimate of yourselves, measuring your value by
> how much faith God has given you. (Romans 12:3, NLT)

The Word of God enjoins us to measure ourselves by how much
faith God has given to us. We have to be honest in our estimate
of ourselves. Do not color that resume. What you have is enough
for God to work with. God is not looking for much but just a
faith like mustard seed. All you have, is all you need.

One day the widow of one of Elisha's fellow prophets came
to Elisha and cried out to him, "My husband who served

you is dead, and you know how he feared the LORD. But now a creditor has come, threatening to take my two sons as slaves." "What can I do to help you?" Elisha asked. "Tell me, what do you have in the house?" "Nothing at all, except a flask of olive oil," she replied. (2 Kings 4:1–2, NLT)

A flask of olive oil is enough to guarantee abundance. This woman had a very important and precious commodity in the home and she thought she had nothing. Most times, we do not value what we have and we waste our time looking for what we do not have. *This is what todays culture |society shows |teaches |conditions.*

Importance of Olive Oil
Used for anointing the body or hair
Used as offering
Used as a fuel in lamps
Used as a medicine
Used to anoint the dead
Used as an article of extensive commerce
Used as a sign of gladness
When omitted, it is a token of sorrow
Not used in sin offering
Not used in jealousy offering

The woman had what she could use for healing, commerce and gladness in her home and she did not realize this. What represents your own olive oil? May the eyes of your understanding be enlightened in Jesus' name.

The step that God will ask you to take to get out of any predicament could be strange, but just follow and trust in him. Do as Mary told the men in John Chapter 2 at the marriage in Cana of Galilee: "Whatsoever he asks you to do just do it." The widow woman in this story was asked to go and borrow; this was the exact problem that got her family into trouble. The trouble starter can become the trouble-shooter. The stone that the builder rejected can end up becoming the chief corner.

Whatever you have is enough. The discarded net of Peter that had been barren all night became what enclosed a great multitude. John Mark that Paul did not want to have any relationship with became the one that was bringing him books. The ways of God are past finding out. His ways are not our ways; neither are His thoughts our thoughts. All you need to do is obey His every word. In that desert that you are in, there is an oasis waiting to be discovered.

Initiate honesty. Be known as one that breathes, talks and walks the honesty walk. Do not be a flip-flop. A man at the end of his tenure asked a question in his farewell address:

> "Then Samuel addressed the people again: "I have done as you asked and given you a king. I have selected him ahead of my own sons, and I stand here, an old, gray-haired man. I have served as your leader since I was a boy. Now tell me as I stand before the LORD and before his anointed one— whose ox or donkey have I stolen? Have I ever cheated any of you? Have I ever oppressed you? Have I ever taken a bribe? Tell me and I will make right whatever I have done wrong." "No," they replied, "you have never cheated or oppressed us in any way, and you have never taken even a single bribe." (1 Samuel 12:1–4, NLT)

Do not go about bootlicking. Be known for your beliefs. This is a trait many Christians fail to display outside the walls of the church. Many Christians have become chameleonic in nature. Christians are trying to mesh in but *"it's the men who walk straight who will settle this land, the women with integrity who will last here"* (Proverbs 2:21, MSG).

In a land where everybody is the same, where all things are fast paced, where it is always zigzag, yo-yo, rat race, always in and out of the microwave, people are still looking for a few peculiar individuals. These are the ones that will stand out in the end. *"The integrity of the upright shall guide them: but the perverseness of transgressors shall destroy them."*(Proverbs 11:3, KJV)

Do not joke with honesty. It confers blessing on your children. *"The godly walk with integrity; blessed are their children after them."*(Proverbs 20:7, NLT)

COMPASSION

Our Lord Jesus Christ has been described with many adjectives, and one that surpasses all others is that he is compassionate. Compassion means concern, kindness, consideration or care. God appreciates a caring heart.

During those days another large crowd gathered. Since they had nothing to eat, Jesus called his disciples to him and said, "I have compassion for these people; they have already been with me three days and have nothing to eat.
(Mark 8:1–2, NIV)

Compassion will lead you to do what others will call crazy. People that are compassionate are able to share. I once heard the story of an old man, and a young man that were both incarcerated because of their belief in Jesus Christ. They were given one meal a day. The old man looked at the young man and realized that he was really finding it difficult to adapt to the menu. The old man was moved with compassion and decided to give the young man a part of his meal. The old man told the young man that he had to pay his tithe even while in prison. We can read the story and say the old man was just obeying the commandment as laid out in the book of Malachi but compassion moved him to fulfill this obligation. Compassion will make you to serve while others want to be served. Compassionate people are not title huggers but trial healers. The word that proceeds out of their mouth is always, "What can we do" or like Jesus said, "Where can we find food for these people?"

A compassionate heart is a sacrificial heart. It is a selfless heart, not a self-serving heart.

When Solomon was made a king, in looking back at his past and the multitude of people he was supposed to lead, he came to two important conclusions: that he did not merit the position (he being a product of adultery, his father was a murderer and the mother an adulteress), and that he had inadequate wisdom to lead the people in his service as a king. He went to God and asked for wisdom to govern them. God granted him more than he requested.

> That night God appeared to Solomon and said to him, "Ask for whatever you want me to give you." Solomon answered God, "You have shown great kindness to David my father and have made me king in his place. Now, LORD God, let your promise to my father David be confirmed, for you have made me king over a people who are as numerous as the dust of the earth. Give me wisdom and knowledge, that I may lead this people, for who is able to govern this great people of yours?" God said to Solomon, "Since this is your heart's desire and you have not asked for wealth, riches or honor, nor for the death of your enemies, and since you have not asked for a long life but for wisdom and knowledge to govern my people over whom I have made you king, therefore wisdom and knowledge will be given you. And I will also give you wealth, riches and honor, such as no king who was before you ever had and none after you will have.
> (2 Chronicle 1:7–12, NIV)

Let us reflect on what God said in the passage above. This man was given a blank check to ask for anything, but he chose wisdom. The wisdom he chose was not to enrich self, devise cunning works, nor be a wolf in sheep's clothing. He chose the wisdom to serve. He wanted to serve out of compassion. Solomon and even Jesus were able to exhibit compassion because of what they have gone through in life. This is not saying that you cannot be compassionate if you have had it easy or smooth in your life. Compassion is a matter of the heart.

> Because God's children are human beings—made of flesh and blood—Jesus also became flesh and blood by being born in human form. For only as a human being could he die, and only by dying could he break the power of the Devil, who had the power of death. Only in this way could he deliver those who have lived all their lives as slaves to the fear of dying. We all know that Jesus came to help the descendants of Abraham, not to help the angels. Therefore, it was necessary for Jesus to be in every respect like us, his brothers and sisters, so that he could be our merciful and faithful High Priest before God. He then could offer a sacrifice that would take away the sins of the people. Since he himself has gone through suffering and temptation, he is able to help us when we are being tempted. (Hebrews 2:14–18, NLT)

As children of God, we all have a wardrobe.

> So, chosen by God for this new life of love, dress in the wardrobe God picked out for you: compassion, kindness...
> (Colossians 3:12, MSG)

In the wardrobe are various outfits and one of them is compassion. Wear the content of your wardrobe so that you can be a winner all the time. Whatever you think you have attained or whoever you think you are, remember it is God that has made it possible. Paul said, "I am what I am by the grace of the Lord."

At a point in the life of David (when he was hiding from Saul), he was in dire straits. He had no food to feed his company, and he appealed to a heart that he thought would be compassionate. *"Ask your young men—they'll tell you. What I'm asking is that you be generous with my men—share the feast! Give whatever your heart tells you to your servants and to me, David your son."* (1 Samuel 25:8, MSG)

He did not realize that there was not a wee bit of compassion in the heart of the man called Nabal. Instead of this man giving a little from what he had, he compounded the situation of David by adding anger to his hunger.

> David's young men went and delivered his message word for word to Nabal. Nabal tore into them, "Who is this David? Who is this son of Jesse? The country is full of runaway servants these days. Do you think I'm going to take good bread and wine and meat freshly butchered for my sheepshearers and give it to men I've never laid eyes on? Who knows where they've come from? (1 Samuel 25:9–11,MSG)

Permit me to advise you this day, when God brings somebody across your way to assist, you do not have to know his origin. The pigmentation of the skin should not influence or debar you from helping. David appealed to Nabal thinking that he had a compassionate heart. Alas, he had a heart of stone. Because the problem of Nabal was that of the heart, he had a heart attack, and he died as a result of this.

> But in the morning, after Nabal had sobered up, she told him the whole story. Right then and there he had a heart attack and fell into a coma. (1 Samuel 25:37, MSG)

Let us ensure that we do good. It is a secret with the Lord. Jesus spoke about compassion in a parable:

For I was hungry, and you didn't feed me. I was thirsty, and you didn't give me anything to drink. I was a stranger, and you didn't invite me into your home. I was naked, and you gave me no clothing. I was sick and in prison, and you didn't visit me.' "Then they will reply, 'Lord, when did we ever see you hungry or thirsty or a stranger or naked or sick or in prison, and not help you?' And he will answer, 'I assure you, when you refused to help the least of these my brothers and sisters, you were refusing to help me.
(Matthew 25:42–45, NLT)

Be kind and compassionate to one another...
(Ephesians 4:32, NIV)

COMMUNICATION

Communication is the ability to articulately relate where you are, what you are about and where you are going to somebody else. On your journey to greatness, communication is very important. You may have the vision of where you are going but it has to be clearly stated and delegated.

How beautiful on the mountains are the feet of those who bring good news. (Isaiah 52:7, NIV)

You have to continually say what you believe in. People may actually start telling you that you are beginning to sound like a broken record. This is the time that the message you are trying to pass across will begin to sink in. A good example is a man called blind Bartimaeus, a beggar. He wanted to pass a simple message of deliverance across to Jesus, but all those around him told him to keep quiet. Instead he screamed the more.

Then they came to Jericho. As Jesus and his disciples, together with a large crowd, were leaving the city, a blind man, Bartimaeus (that is, the Son of Timaeus), was sitting by the roadside begging. When he heard that it was Jesus of Nazareth, he began to shout, "Jesus, Son of David, have mercy on me!" Many rebuked him and told him to be quiet, but he shouted all the more, "Son of David, have mercy on me!" Jesus stopped and said, "Call him." So they called to the blind man, "Cheer up! On your feet! He's calling you." Throwing his cloak aside, he jumped to his feet and came to Jesus. "What do you want me to do for you?" Jesus asked him. The blind man said, "Rabbi, I want to see." "Go," said Jesus, "your faith has healed you." Immediately he received his sight and followed Jesus along the road.

(Mark 10: 46–52, NIV)

If you believe it, shout it because you will soon see it.

Children are wonderful communicators. When children have a need, they will definitely get the message across. If a young child still using diapers is in a room and he feels like answering the call of nature, he will do it wherever he is. The smell of the pooh will attract the attention of either the parents or those in the room. Hear this, if the smell does not spring the parents to action and the child is uncomfortable, he is going to scream, and the scream will simply mean, "I need you to change my diapers." It does not matter how many people are in a room, if a young child needs something and he does not get it on time, you can take this to the bank, he is going to scream.

I attended a wedding recently. During the reception, a young girl of about two-and-a-half-years-old was sitting at a table with her mother. She wanted food, but her table was not being served on time. She did something to correct the situation. Your guess is as good as mine as to what she did.

On one occasion my wife promised our children that she would buy tim bits (little doughnuts) for them from Tim Hortons (a popular Canadian doughnut store chain). I did not know this, and we all packed ourselves into our mini van to attend a wedding. As we approached a Tim Hortons store, the cry of tim bits came on strong, but I ignored it. We got to the venue of the wedding, spent some time there, and proceeded to go back home. As we approached this Tim Hortons store again, the cry of the children became a chorus. I still tried to ignore the cry but our youngest son said, "I do not like Mummy...." My wife immediately told me to drive into the Tim Hortons.

In effective communications, sometimes we have to say it as it is, no sugar-coating, no watering it down. There is a time to say with faith that it is well and there is a time to tell God, "Lord you have to arise on my behalf, or else I am dead meat." In the same vein, in our day-to-day dealings at home, and in our offices, sometimes we have to say it is not okay because whatever we do not confront, we will not correct, and whatever we do not face will not flee.

Resist the devil and he will flee from you. (James 4:7, KJV)

At creation in the book of Genesis, after the birds, light, sea, firmament, etc., were created, God admired the work of His hands by saying, "it is good." After the creation of man He said, "it is not good for man to be alone." He then corrected the situation by creating woman from the rib of man.

Tom Peters said in the article "Leadership Is Confusing As Hell:"

Leadership takes an almost bottomless supply of verbal energy: working the phones, staying focused on your message, repeating the same mantra until you can't stand the sound of your own voice—and then repeating it some more, because just when you start to become bored witless with the message, it's probably starting to seep into the organization.

One of the reasons why you have to keep on repeating it is to take away any internal doubt within yourself and also to convince the people that you want to key into the vision that not only do you mean what you are saying, but you also know where you are going. You are not a flip-flop.

Communication is not only asking people to do something, but letting them know why they need to do what you are asking them to do. The opportunity cost of doing what is being asked, are the alternatives that needs to be forgone. Your objective must be clearly explained.

It must not always be a case of "if you do not do it, fire and brimstone will fall."

People have difficulties, and they want to identify with somebody that has gone through or is going through what they are experiencing. We often project perfection while people want to identify with our weakness. Even when we do administer bitter herbs, let us do it with a golden spoon. In communicating, you have to be prepared to hear negative things. It may be about yourself or about what you are doing. This assists in personal appraisal. For many companies, at least once or twice a year there is what is called a performance appraisal. The manager or supervisor sits with a subordinate and reviews the performance based on laid down criteria.

This is something that we should do with ourselves. Jesus Christ encourages it.

"What are people saying about who the Son of Man is?"(Matthew 16:13, MSG)

The idea behind this is not to allow yourself to be pulled down or distracted from your goal, but it is to allow you to ask yourself, "Am I passing the right message across?" The simple criterion is objectivity—on the part of the person asking the question. This is to ensure that the answer to the question enable him to take an inward look at his activities—*insight.* We shall extensively examine this in the next chapter. If you are doing it right, there could be lots of criticism and praise singers, but God

True humility

will always set somebody apart to tell you the whole truth and nothing but the truth.

Simon Peter responded to Jesus inquiry:

> You're the Christ, the Messiah, the Son of the living God." Jesus came back, "God bless you, Simon, son of Jonah! You didn't get that answer out of books or from teachers. My Father in heaven, God Himself, let you in on this secret of who I really am. (Matthew 16:1–17, MSG)

My prayer to you is that on your journey to greatness, God is going to let you in on this secret of who you really are because you need at least somebody outside of your nuclear family to believe in your mantra. There was a king called Ahab, and all he wanted to listen to were people that would speak with enticing words of man's wisdom, people that would scratch his itch, people that would fan the embers of his ego, pushing him in the process towards destruction. In all this, according to the benevolence of God, he still set apart one man that God would use to show the secret of who Ahab really was.

Alas, Ahab did not like the picture presented, but instead of making amends, he locked up this man in jail.

> So Micaiah told him, "In a vision I saw all Israel scattered on the mountains, like sheep without a shepherd. And the LORD said, 'Their master has been killed. Send them home in peace. (2 Chronicles 18:16, NLT)

Communication requires feedback. Is the feedback moving you closer to what God intends for your life or are you ignoring the feedback?

Feedback ignored is furor ignited.

In our homes, our children need to know where we are headed. We need to carry them along, especially if they are old enough to understand. Do not meet their request with an anger-laden retort. If you are planning to buy a home, change jobs or whatsoever you are planning to do, they should be part of the process inasmuch as they can understand. God does not keep things from his children. God told Abraham about what is going to happen to Sodom. We must imbibe the same characteristic.

When God asked Abraham to go and sacrifice Isaac, Abraham explained to Isaac that they would be sacrificing in the land of Moriah. As they proceeded and Isaac did not see any lamb or ram to be used in the sacrifice he asked Dad, "I can see the knife and the wood but there is no lamb." Abraham replied that God would provide himself a lamb (speaking prophetically because Jesus was provided later).

Had it been some of us parents, we would sharply retort with our eyes blazing with fire and brimstone, "Shut up, you talk too much. A child should know when to keep quiet; you do not interfere in what you have not been called into," raving and ranting on and on.

Please remember this; effective communication leads to good choice-making. One of the reasons why some of our children take the wrong turn is because they do not have any benchmark or yardstick. As parents, we sometimes say nothing to our children. Their mind is like a sponge, it wants to soak up information. If you do not take time to instruct your children, they will seek tutoring elsewhere. This may be contrary and detrimental to your belief as a Christian. When we effectively communicate with our children, when they have to choose between the gun and God, the syringe and the Savior or Hollywood and the Holy Spirit, they will immediately know the best option. The mind is either correctly or incorrectly informed. If incorrectly informed, it leads to, "Had I known." When a man says this, it is already too late. May it not be too late for you in Jesus' name. Amen.

The God that we serve informs us, which gives us the ability to make a choice.

Now listen! Today I am giving you a choice between prosperity and disaster, between life and death..."Today I have given you the choice between life and death, between blessings and curses. I call on heaven and earth to witness the choice you make. Oh, that you would choose life, that you and your descendants might live!
(Deuteronomy 30:15,19, NLT)

In the Garden of Eden, he took Adam on a stroll and showed him what he should and should not do. Adam and Eve later made their choice.

Communication births options. The options will clearly state the advantages and the disadvantages of whichever option that you choose. Communicate your vision of greatness. You are a book in writing. There is an expectation for your manifestation. You are the will of God in revelation. People have paid top dollar to see you perform. The created world can hardly wait for your appearance. Do not bottle up that gift or novel idea. Shout it loud.

COURAGE

A major preoccupation of Satan as he goes about seeking whom to devour is to kill, to steal and to destroy your ability to make informed decisions. Before he can accomplish this, he needs the cooperation of your mind.

In whom the god of this world hath blinded the minds of them. (2 Corinthians 4:4, KJV)

i.e. T.V's, phones, advertisment, etc.

There is always a great battle going on for the control of your mind. The kingdom of darkness wants to use created being to discredit God. An avenue to accomplish this is by allowing thoughts that negates the existence of God to filter into the human mind. This is the reason why Satan wanted to take control of the mind of Job so that Job can curse God or in simple words say there is no God. It is only the foolish that will say there is no God. The devil will attempt to sow seeds of discord and fear in your mind. Fear leads to worry, and worry is nothing other than borrowed trouble. Worry is taking a load that is not yours upon yourself. The Word of God says you should cast all your cares upon Jesus, for he cares for you. The fear of tomorrow will empty the strength to do anything meaningful today.

Fear is a paralyzer. It will attempt to prevent you from taking a meaningful step. This kind of person will always be hedging; he will neither be hot nor cold and he will end up being spewed out. Fear is a strong man that needs to be bound.

It really is. Thank you God for bringing me out of that.

How in the world do you think it's possible in broad daylight to enter the house of an awake, able-bodied man and walk off with his possessions unless you tie him up first? Tie him up, though, and you can clean him out. (Matthew 12:29, MSG)

To clean out fear, you must first bind up fear. Fear is garbage that needs to be collected and dumped in the dumpsite. After sweeping garbage, you dump it in a garbage bag, tie up the bag and then throw it into the garbage truck for onward transmission to a dumpsite. There are a couple of things that both the disposer and the collector ensure—securing of the garbage bag and securing of the garbage truck.

This is to ensure that the garbage that has been swept from the house or the street is not spilled. This is exactly the way to treat fear. It is garbage that must be tied up by the Word of God.

Fear will not allow you to follow the leading of the Lord.

For I the **LORD** thy God will hold thy right hand, saying unto thee, Fear not; I will help thee. Fear not, thou worm Ja-

cob, and ye men of Israel; I will help thee, saith the LORD, and thy redeemer, the Holy One of Israel.
(Isaiah 41:13–14, KJV)

God has promised to help you and neither to leave or forsake you. God is extending his right arm of righteousness to all his children but fear is not making us to hold unto him. Listen to this, God knows your inadequacies, he called Jacob a worm. He knows every fiber of your being; your substance was not and is not hid from him.

You need to be courageous. In any situation that you find yourself, create a shield of courage against every fiery dart because God has wonderful plans for you, and until you display and embody courage, you will not get it. Cowards die many times before their death. Courageous people are a terror to the kingdom of darkness. After every disappointment, they are able to tell the devil, "Is that all?" Do not allow fear to hold you back. *"Fear not, little flock; for it is your Father's good pleasure to give you the kingdom"*(Luke 12:32, KJV).

In your quest for greatness there will be times when you will fast and pray and it will seem as if God is silent to your pleas and supplication, but be of good cheer. No matter how hard the prince of Persia will try, the answer will still come.

Then he said, "Don't be afraid, Daniel. Since the first day you began to pray for understanding and to humble yourself before your God, your request has been heard in heaven. I have come in answer to your prayer. (Daniel 10:12, NLT)

Say to those who are afraid, "Be strong, and do not fear, for your God is coming to destroy your enemies. He is coming to save you. (Isaiah 35:4, NLT)

The major reason why the devil uses fear as a weapon against the children of God is because we have the power to make our way prosperous. He wants us to be confused and lose our kingship authority and royal identity. So that instead of us seeing victory and might, we see vanquished and minute. He uses fear to cause confusion so that we will be threading wheat in the winepress.

For anybody that has done a little bit of chemistry, you will know that there are three states of matter—solid, liquid, gas. Leave a solid object in a place and you will meet it there after a long time except somebody or something moves the object. For a liquid, the speed of travel is very slow compared to gas or the gaseous state. If somebody is cooking, before you see the meal, you would have smelled it.

Fear can be likened to a gas, it travels very wide and it permeates any environment where it is allowed to take root. If you talk to somebody that is overwhelmed with fear, you can smell it in all that he says. Fear is a spirit, and the Word of God expressly states what he has given us.

> For God has not given us a spirit of fear, but of power and of love and of a sound mind. (2 Timothy 1:7, NKJV)

Do not allow Satan to take control of your mind. Use the Word of God to bind Satan. God and the elders of Israel had to repeatedly tell Joshua to be of good courage, but talking alone will not cut it. You have to do something else—study the Word of God. This is the ammunition that you need to combat fear. Joshua was advised to not only read the Word but to also meditate on it, to uproot fear so that he would have good success.

> Even if others will not.
>
> Be strong and very courageous. Be careful to obey all the law my servant Moses gave you; do not turn from it to the right or to the left, that you may be successful wherever you go. Do not let this Book of the Law depart from your mouth; meditate on it day and night, so that you may be careful to do everything written in it. Then you will be prosperous and

successful. Have I not commanded you? Be strong and courageous. Do not be terrified; do not be discouraged, for the LORD your God will be with you wherever you go. (Joshua 1:7–9, NIV)

What you allow to come into your heart will determine what will come out of you. *"Above all else, guard your heart, for it affects everything you do"* (Proverbs 4:23, NLT).

Be diligent in protecting your heart. *"Keep thy heart with all diligence; for out of it are the issues of life"* (Proverbs 4:23, KJV).

This is highly underestimated.

HOW DO YOU INITIATE?

To initiate or start anything, there has to be a conviction. Daniel said, "I will not defile myself with the portion of the king's meat." He furthermore prayed when the commandment came from the king of Babylon that nobody should pray. He was convinced of the power of God. You do not have to be super talented to initiate. It simply means starting. If you are planning to start a business and you have done your due diligence with everything pointing to a glorious outcome, then start. The world is full of people that failed to start. The people that fail to initiate ultimately become the servants of those that initiated.

WHEN DO YOU INITIATE?

The answer is now. You cannot wait till you have before giving. A man that does not pay his tithe while earning $1,000 will not pay his tithe when he starts earning $10,000. One of the hardest changes that I had to make while paying tithe was to pay on my gross earnings, not net earnings. It was tough initially, but since I started doing it, I have not looked back. I recognize the principle of counting the cost so that you do not abandon the project halfway. This should not be used as an excuse. If all those people that have a successful business waited till everything was "in place" before they started, they would be nowhere today.

NUGGETS

- In order for one not to vegetate, one must move forward (progression), as God abhors stagnancy.
- The first step is usually the hardest in any endeavor or enterprise.
- Initiative is the ability to either do what others have not done or to improve on what others have done (that is, to add value).
- God has given us talents each according to his/her own ability. This gifting leads to lifting.
- Everything that you start must be led by God.
- There are certain things that one is forbidden to initiate:
  - Do not initiate a lie.
  - Do not initiate confusion.
  - What you should initiate:
  - Honesty—The hallmark of any great endeavor is what it is founded on. What you have is enough for God to work with.
  - Compassion—God appreciates a caring heart. Compassion will make you serve while others want to be served. A compassionate heart is a sacrificial heart.
  - Communication—the ability to articulately relate where you are, what you are about, and where you are going to somebody else. If you believe in something, you must shout it, because you will soon see its physical manifestation. Communication requires feedback, and feedback ignored is furor ignited. Effective communication leads to good choice-making. Communication births options.
  - Courage—Fear leads to worry, and worry is nothing other than borrowed trouble. To clear fear, you must first bind

it up. Courageous people are a terror to the kingdom of darkness.

- When do you initiate: The answer is now!

PRAYER POINTS

- Lord, the circumstances I need to create to achieve greatness, lead me to them and help me create them, in Jesus' name.
- In Jesus' name, I refuse to be stagnant. I choose to move forward. I choose to grow. Father, enlarge my coast in greatness.
- My God, correct everything that is sluggish, inert, inactive or dormant in my life. Let your quickening Spirit that made Jesus resurrect quicken every situation in my life.
- Holy Spirit, please correct everything that is without form and becoming an empty waste in my life, and enlighten my darkness; in Jesus' name.
- Lord, I hear your word to every situation in my life that is in a sleeping position, saying "Get up." I now arise to shine in Jesus' name! Amen.
- My King, I choose to stir up your gifts in me, to initiate that which you have given unto me now, to give birth to my God-given dream, because it will live and many will take shelter under its wings.
- Lord, I choose to add value that is in high demand. Help me not to initiate lies and confusion, but to be a mirror that brightly reflects the glory of God.
- My God, give me a heart of compassion. You are lifting me up because of your compassion. Help me to lift up others in compassion.
- O Lord, enable me to communicate effectively and carry along all I need to carry along.
- I rebuke every spirit of fear in Jesus' name; I have the Spirit of power, of love and a sound mind.

INSIGHT

Lots of people miss opportunity because it is covered in overalls and looks like work. . . . Farmer of seeds
- Thomas Edison

...grew until he became very great: (Genesis 26:13, KJV)

Insight is a deep perception of a situation. It is the clear understanding of a complex condition or grasping the inner nature of things. It includes an understanding of the motives and reasons behind one's actions. Insight is an ability to look inward—deep calling unto the deep.

Life with all its intricacies can be complex but an insight can make life simple and exciting. A whole lot of people have fallen into drudgery and are mired in the rut of life, thereby living a listless and colorless life. All that they do is to go, grow and glow in complaining while all God expects in creating us is to go, grow and glow in His love. It is time for the children of God to have an insight into what they are (I am what I am by the grace of God) by looking inside their house. Your destiny must be redeemed and dominion restored.

A LOOK INSIDE YOUR HOUSE

In life, one of the places that a man often neglects to look at for solution to any problem is inward. A whole lot of people often look outside to blame others or the laid down systems of the world. For any man or family that desires growth, there has to be a constant inward looking—insight. You focus on developing your strength and destroying your weakness.

Man is a spirit that lives in a body (tent) by the avenue of the soul. The body houses or provides accommodation for the spirit and the soul. The spirit of man serves as a link or conduit for the receiving and translation of information from the Holy Spirit. The information received by the spirit is now relayed to the soul or mind to make decisions.

> But there is a spirit in man: and the inspiration of the Almighty giveth them understanding. (Job 32:8, KJV)

This spirit of man has to reside in a house (body) that is conducive for edification and elevation. If the spirit of man is restless or uncomfortable, then information from the Holy Spirit will be intermittent or non-existent. Consequently, the mind will be incorrectly informed. For man to be able to speak words of wisdom or words of knowledge, the house (body) must be conducive.

The body of man is the house.

A house is a dwelling place, tent or shelter. In government, a house is a place where laws are enacted. Household means the inhabitants of the house (i.e. those that live in the house for shelter and to pass laws). Since the house is a place where laws are passed, strange and strangulating laws will be passed if the dwellers in the house are not in harmony.

God understands the importance of a house or household to the growth and development of the people that he has formed to show forth his praise. This is the reason why the body (house) was not omitted when He said through the mouth of Apostle Paul, "*May God himself, the God of peace, sanctify you through and through. May your whole spirit, soul and body be kept blameless at the coming of our Lord Jesus Christ*" (1 Thessalonians 5:23, NIV).

The spirit, soul and body have to be in harmony for the law of the spirit of life to be effective. Out of the three, the weakest is the body, but it also holds a significant position because it is the medium without which we will not be having signs and wonders today. If there is no human body, there will be no people. The Holy Spirit may want to move, but the assistance of a cooperative body is needed.

This is the reason why Satan sought the assistance of Eve in the Garden of Eden when he tried to subvert the course of mankind, and Jesus had to come in human flesh to put things back in order. Jesus made an important, deep and far reaching pronouncement that a man's enemy will be those of his own household.

A man's enemies will be the members of his own household. (Matthew 10:36, NIV)

He was speaking from knowledge. Three women helped in preserving the Israelites from slaughter by Pharaoh of Egypt. God made a proclamation concerning them:

And because the midwives revered and feared God, He made them households [of their own]. (Exodus 1:21, TAB)

And it came to pass, because the midwives feared God, that He made them houses. (Exodus 1:21, KJV)

Some other translations say God gave them families of their own. There is nowhere that you have it recorded that these midwives were barren or had no husbands. If you take a peek back into the olden days, the people that were given the responsibilities of midwives were those with experience in the art of delivering babies. This is primarily because they had children of their own. They understood the pain, pangs and pleasures of childbirth.

Therefore, what the Word of God is trying to say is that God removed desolation from these women and made them habitable. There was peace and harmony in their homes and their children and husbands excelled. The husband, wife and children were able to live together as a cohesive family unit. This confirms the Word of God.

> And my people shall dwell in a peaceable habitation, and in sure dwellings, and in quiet resting places;
> (Isaiah 32:18, KJV)

One of the things that Jesus emphasised while on earth to assure us that it is well with us is a promise of a beautiful mansion in heaven. "

> In my Father's house are many mansions: if it were not so, I would have told you. I go to prepare a place for you.
> (John 14:2, KJV) Thanks God & Jesus but... I don't want a mansion for myself. I want to live w you, Babe, Lex, my

The importance of a peaceful, loving and harmonious dwelling parents, cannot be overstated. The Most High God realized that for man to be all that he intends them to be, their house, tent or body must be in great condition. To ensure this, God did something significant.

> And the **LORD** God formed a man's body from the dust of the ground and breathed into it the breath of life. And the man became a living person. (Genesis 2:7, **NLT**)

It is because of this singular act that the children of God are referred to as a spiritual house, "*Ye also, as lively stones, are built up a spiritual house...*"(1Peter 2: 5, KJV*).*

As children of God, we have been "in–powered" (breath into) for excellence with the breath of life by God into us, we were given a dose of the nature of the Most High God. The concept of "in–powerment" simply means there is no contaminant and it is not extraneous. What God gave to us was pure, undiluted and very important. We became partakers of the divine nature.

We are now a special dwelling place, but remember that a man's enemies will be the members of his own household. This statement emphasises that growth begins from the inside. What is in your house (body) that is preventing the household from flourishing? Paul the Apostle cried out concerning his body (house) and the members of the body (household).

> But I see another law at work in the members of my body, waging war against the law of my mind and making me a prisoner of the law of sin at work within my members. (Romans 7:23, NIV)

It is those things that live inside us that will prevent us from being great, not those things outside of us. Those that reside in a house can either cause the house to be a home or hell. A house is supposed to be a dwelling for treasure not turmoil.

> Then said he unto them, Therefore every scribe which is instructed unto the kingdom of heaven is like unto a man that is an householder, which bringeth forth out of his treasure things new and old. (Matthew 13:52, KJV)

To be instructed means to be trained, coached, tutored and educated. If you build on this, it means something valuable had been deposited by the tutor into the pupil. It is now up to the pupil to use what is on the inside, if correctly imbibed and inculcated, to be excellent in life. What is supposed to showcase us has been etched or engraved into us. It lives on the inside of us. *"But we have this treasure in earthen vessels"* (2 Corinthians 4:7, KJV).

To all those that are reading this book, there is treasure on the inside of you; take a deep look inward. Be insightful. An inward look allowed Isaac to grow and also know the source of his growth.

The Bible says Isaac grew; how did Isaac grow? The word "grow" can mean to expand, increase, become more evident or develop. The definition that really captures the process of growth is *to come into existence from a source.* Growth originates from a source. When you look at a tree, there is a part of the tree that is not always visible, but the strength, nourishment and continued development of the tree depends on this part called a root.

The root of a tree is usually the underground portion of a plant and serves as support. It draws minerals and water from the surrounding soil and sometimes stores food. The root is the source. The tree makes sure that the source is not neglected so that it does not wither. *As a child of God, you have a source that can never be dry.*

In growing, Isaac gave reverence to the one that can make him grow. He looked inward and saw that Emmanuel lives in him. *Insight will help in identifying what you need to do to keep on growing, why you have not been growing or how you need to grow.*

It does not matter the amount of fertilizer that a farmer applies to a rice stalk, it will not transform it to a maize cob. Rice already has its genetic constituent. The external application of fertilizer will not change the internal constitution.

The same thing applies to every man; if you have been wired or genetically constituted to be a dwarf, no amount of growth pills will turn you to a giant. The good news concerning you today is that you have been **genetically put together to be the head and not the tail**, to be **above only and not beneath.** The solution to your growth lies inside. It lies with the one that has put you together and is living in you. Look inward, let there be insight. When you became born again, you became a Christian that is Christ like. You carry Christ around in you every moment. For

Christ in you is the hope of glory, not shame. For growth, Isaac looked inside the house and made an amazing discovery.

THE CONTENT OF YOUR HOUSE

An amazing discovery that Isaac made was that God was inside of him and living in him. This God that is living on the inside of him is called the Almighty.

> ...I am God Almighty. (Genesis 17:1, KJV)

The concept of the Almighty implies that somebody has absolute power. Nobody can question what He does and what He does not do. God is the Almighty. God has absolute power. He can give whatever he wants to anybody, His resources are endless and He can never go bankrupt. God cannot be limited. He is called by the name Jehovah. He is the glory and the lifter-up. He sits on the circuits of the earth and beholds the inhabitants as grasshoppers.

He breathes and the mountain skips. He speaks and the earth melts. He is the refuge and fortress, the ever-present help in times of trouble. He separated the red sea by the blast of the breath of His nostrils. He speaks and it is done. He commands and it stands fast. Nobody gave power to Him; therefore nobody can take it from Him. He is the silencer of every coup plotter. He is called the Ancient Of Days. He upholds everything by the word of His power. He is the truth; therefore He can never lie. He is the way; with Him you can never be lost. He is the owner and origin of power.

"Jehovah Shammeka (The Lord Thy Keeper). The **LORD** is thy keeper: the **LORD** is thy shade upon thy right hand (Psalms 121:5). God calls Himself the Keeper of His people. David had experienced the keeping power of God through the various crises in his life. Jehovah Shammeka promised Jacob that He will keep him as he went into a land where he had not been before. The same God can be your keeper. When the path is dangerous and you think you cannot make it to the end, there is One who can keep your foot from slipping. When other people think there is no more hope for you, you can trust in Jehovah Shammeka to uphold you with His mighty power. When plans are being made to destroy you, you can believe God to be your watchman. He will send His angel to keep you all the way and bring you to the place He has prepared for you. *Wow, thank you Lord for this answer.*

Sept 1st 20 22

When the enemies of your life think they have done their worst, you can be rest assured that no weapon formed against you shall prosper. Your keeper is stronger than their plans and strategies. He will keep you from the terror of the night and from the arrow that flies by day because He is the Keeper who does not sleep nor slumber. With God as your keeper, the devil cannot do you any hurt. The LORD is able to bless you and keep you and make His face to shine upon you and give you His peace. His name is Jehovah Shammeka, the LORD Thy Keeper."

- Excerpt taken from 70 Names of God by Dr. Tai Ikomi

An inward look or insight will make sure that you are connected to Him. If you have not yet surrendered to Him or your life and conduct does not glorify His name, you should know that God is great and He is of great power. When Isaac found out that the almighty was in him and with him, he also realized the awesome power of the almighty. As a child of God, Emmanuel lives in you. Below are the things that the Almighty God can do.

GOD HAS THE POWER TO REDEEM AND RESCUE.

He is calling unto you. He does not want you to be lonely anymore. He wants to be your friend. He is a friend that **neither leaves nor forsakes**. When you surrender to Him, He will do more than any parent for you. God is able to redeem you from shame and in exchange give you a part of his glory.

> But God will redeem my life from the grave; he will surely take me to himself. (Psalm 49:15, NIV)

In the goodness and infinite mercy of God, He **saved us from destruction**. When we were dead in our sins, He **redeemed us**. To redeem means to recover ownership. This implies that we were formerly owned by the devil through the avenue of sin, and a recovery had to be done. This recovery took a huge process. For example, if you purchase an item, before you bought that thing it must have some worth. It must be relatively precious when it was bought. When you now become the owner of the item, it will have some value to you.

When we were in the camp of the devil, we were precious to the kingdom of darkness to help in furthering the work of darkness and derailing those that are in the light. Do you know what? Some of us really succeeded in getting recruits into the enemy's camp and making a shipwreck of the faith of some that were believers in Christ. We were mired in the clay of destruction and defeat.

Despite all those things that we were doing then, we did not know that Satan who was **our master,** had been **defeated**. This is because Jesus Christ pronounced that He saw Satan falling down as lightning from the sky. So we were also in effect defeated by reason of association. We were actually losing while we had the deranged opinion that we were winning. We saw ourselves as a success. As many as are in the devil's camp have been pro-grammed for destruction. The only thing that has been keeping them going is that God in His mercy has not allowed them to press the destruct button yet. The good thing is that some of us opted by the grace of God for the button of life at the time ap-pointed, because a decision was made when it pleased the most high God to buy us back.

To buy us back implied that a higher price had to be paid by the one doing the buyback. The price was the blood of Jesus. It took Jesus laying down His life and shedding His blood, because the life of the flesh is in the blood. Let me expand more on the concept of buyback. In the days of slavery, when a master bought a slave, he branded the slave. In some cases a sort of mark was placed on the body of the slave to make sure that they only ate when he wanted them to eat. A hole was made in the upper and lower lips, and a padlock was used to seal their mouth.

When we were bought back, all these marks were eliminat-ed, and a new mark was placed upon us that identifies us as to who we belong to.

> But the firm foundation of (laid by) God stands, sure and unshaken, bearing this seal (inscription): The Lord knows those who are His, and, Let everyone who names [himself by] the name of the Lord give up all iniquity and stand aloof from it. (2 Timothy 2:19, TAB)

This new mark not only announces who we belong to, but it also wards off enemies from attacking us.

> From henceforth let no man trouble me: for I bear in my body the marks of the Lord Jesus. (Galatians 6:17, KJV)

Jesus not only redeemed us, or bought us back, he also rescued us from defeat. In a competition where medals are given—gold, silver and bronze—the competitors that are first, second and third gets the aforementioned medals respectively. There are some key things: the other participants do not get a medal, and they do not mount the podium; the one that won stands on the higher podium.

The above example deals with a competition that involves more than two. In the competition between the kingdom of darkness and light, the winner takes it all. The good thing is that Jesus had already taken it all. Hallelujah. After He was crucified on the cross and put in the tomb, He went to hades, sheol and took the keys of death and hell from the devil. He also freed all the patriarchs that had been held in captivity. This is why the Word of God can say, "death where is your sting and grave where is your victory?" Jesus Christ redeemed you into the winning camp and rescued you from defeat. You have been raised to sit in heavenly places with Christ Jesus far above principalities and powers.

GOD HAS THE POWER TO ELIMINATE YOUR ENEMIES

When we talk about enemies, it is not your next door neighbor or your boss or colleague in the office (in some cases the devil may be using them). In this context, sickness, anger, lies, frivolous living, debt, discouragement, defeat, fear, etc., are enemies of greatness. God is more than able to nullify all these nemeses.

Imagine a boxing bout and a contender throwing in the towel after constant pummeling. God will pummel your enemies to submission in Jesus' name.

> Say unto God, How terrible art thou in thy works! through the greatness of thy power shall thine enemies submit themselves unto thee. (Psalm 66:3, KJV)

Look at this beautiful account in the Word of God. It is about the Israelites in Egypt. God met a man by the name of Moses in the wilderness and said, "go and tell Pharaoh to let my people (the Israelites) go to worship me." Pharaoh did not hearken. His heart was hardened. But by the greatness of the power of God, he temporarily submitted. By the time he saw the handiwork of God in the form of plagues that culminated in the death of every first born in Egypt, while the dwellers of "Goshen" were spared, he finally allowed the Israelites to go.

Like all diehards, he did not give up totally. He changed his mind and pursued the Israelites. But he ended up perishing in the red sea. The enemies of the Israelites perished.

One of the reasons why we still have enemies in the form of debt, anger, lies and turbulence is because we are not following the prescribed route of God. We have not taken them to the red sea. In case you are wondering how to do that, this story will let you have a peek.

There was a woman that was constantly fighting with the husband and she then decided to go and use voodoo to arrest the man. On getting to the house of the voodoo man who happened to be a wise man, she recounted her problem. This man gave her a medication with the instruction on how to use it. This woman had the opportunity to test the medication the following evening when a disagreement occurred with the husband. She went to the room and put the medication in her mouth and the instruction given was to chew on the medication when there is strife. As she was chewing, the husband was speaking angrily. At a point the husband stopped and went out of the room. This woman was ecstatic that the medication was working. She tried it again and again, and what she noticed each time was that the length of time that it took for the argument to stop kept diminishing until the husband asked what has come over her. That was how the constant fighting stopped.

The voodoo man, after listening to the explanation of the woman and the situation in the home, realized that the woman needed to imbibe patience just like it is recorded in the book of James to "let patience have her perfect work, that ye may be perfect and entire, wanting nothing." She also bridled her tongue.

> For in many things we offend all. If any man offend not in word, the same is a perfect man, and able also to bridle the whole body. (James 3:2, KJV)

What this woman had to take to the red sea was impatience and the fire that spews from her mouth. The medication that the voodoo man gave her was a huge wad of absorbent cotton to chew on always. With the huge wad of absorbent cotton, the woman would not be able to speak. Peace was then restored to her home. Whatever you are going through, take it to Jesus, the Word of God. He sent His word to heal and deliver from destruction.

WHAT A FRIEND WE HAVE IN JESUS

Text: Joseph M. Scriven, 1820–1886

1. What a friend we have in Jesus,
all our sins and griefs to bear!
What a privilege to carry
everything to God in prayer!
O what peace we often forfeit,
O what needless pain we bear,
all because we do not carry
everything to God in prayer.

2. Have we trials and temptations?
Is there trouble anywhere?
We should never be discouraged;
take it to the Lord in prayer.
Can we find a friend so faithful
who will all our sorrows share?

Jesus knows our every weakness;
take it to the Lord in prayer.

3. Are we weak and heavy laden,
cumbered with a load of care?
Precious Savior, still our refuge;
take it to the Lord in prayer.
Do thy friends despise, forsake thee?
Take it to the Lord in prayer!
In his arms he'll take and shield thee;
thou wilt find a solace there.

One of the things that we neglect to do is to take it (our problems) to God. Instead of taking it to God in prayer, we take it to people for guidance.

> Casting the whole of your care [all your anxieties, all your worries, all your concerns, once and for all] on Him, for He cares for you affectionately and cares about you watchfully. (1 Peter 5:7, **TAB**)

Sometimes we do take our situations to the altar but when we are leaving we carry it with us again instead of leaving it behind. Hear the testimony of David when you take it once and for all to him.

> I WILL bless the Lord at all times; His praise shall continually be in my mouth. My life makes its boast in the Lord; let the humble and afflicted hear and be glad. O magnify the Lord with me, and let us exalt His name together. I sought (inquired of) the Lord and required Him [of necessity and on the authority of His Word], and He heard me, and delivered me from all my fears. They looked to Him and were radiant; their faces shall never blush for shame or be confused. (Psalm 34:1–5, **TAB**)

GOD HAS THE POWER
TO CALM EVERY CALAMITY

An amazing thing about God is the ability to wipe away tears. There is the story of a widow woman with an only child (a boy). The boy died, and they were about to bury the boy. This woman's only hope of amounting to anything in life was the boy. She had spent money on his education, only for death to snatch victory from this woman but Jesus showed up on the scene. The show-up God will show up for you and show forth in your life in Jesus' name. Every stormy situation in your life will receive the peace of God, in Jesus' name. Amen.

> By his power the sea grew calm. By his skill he crushed the great sea monster. (Job 26:12, NLT)

In life we go through situations that make us wonder where God is. Is God alive at all? If he is, how come I am facing such situations and how come he is not doing anything about it? Gideon said something similar "If God be for us why are all these things befalling us, if God be for us where are all the promises he made to our fore-fathers."

I was speaking to a brother in Christ that I have not heard from in about three weeks after leaving several messages. I fully know that his family was going through some challenging situations. Finally he gave me a call and he started recounting what transpired a couple of days back. He said as he stepped out of the house, he looked up and asked, "God what is the meaning of all these, how come my children have all these health issues, where is your face in all these?"

Lastly he said he asked God, "What has happened to all the prayers that are being said to you not only by me and my wife but by other friends." He said he heard God's response audibly, "If not for the prayers, something else would have happened."

In all he said, he could still thank God. The response from God gave him the strength to keep moving on; calm came over him.

GOD HAS THE POWER
TO EXALT EVERY EXILED

Are you displaced or banished? You are a candidate for a lifting up from God. He knows what to teach you to become somebody in life. A man by the name Joseph the son of Israel was thrown into prison but right there in prison, God taught him the interpretation of the dream of a king and he was made a prime minister.

> Behold, God exalteth by his power: who teacheth like him? (Job 36:22, KJV)

In whatever way you think you have been set aside or forsaken, God is able to seek you out. The stone that the builders reject can still be the head corner. Mordecai and Esther were exiles, but Mordecai prepared and trained Esther properly, and she won a beauty contest, thereby becoming the queen. At a time when Mordecai should be enjoying the privilege of having somebody in the corridor of power, calamity struck. A man by the name Haman conspired to have all the Israeli nationals wiped out. The Almighty did something about it because the gallows that Haman built to hang Mordecai was used in hanging him. The impending calamity became celebration. Hitherto you have been tolerated; henceforth you shall be celebrated in Jesus' name.

I once heard the story of a young boy (those we call a nerd) that was ridiculed by peers because all he could do was read and read. He had an unusual way of dressing with his thick glasses. One day he got fed up with the constant ridicule and he decided to end it all as the account goes. He packed all his books in his knapsack on a Friday so that his parents wouldn't have to clear the mess when he was gone.

On his way home he encountered a classmate that decided to take an interest in him (a divine connection), and this young man invited him out the next day. This was a pleasant surprise for this boy because he had not experienced such kindness in a while. Due to this act, he shelved the idea of committing suicide. On the day of graduation, as the valedictorian he was asked to give a speech. He then recounted what happened on that fateful Friday. The exiled by peers became exalted by friends, foes and families. The dream is not over yet.

GOD HAS POWER TO FEED THE FAMISHED

> Every man also to whom God hath given riches and wealth, and hath given him power to eat thereof, and to take his portion, and to rejoice in his labour; this is the gift of God. (Ecclesiastes 5:19, KJV)

One of the things that some of us take lightly is the power to eat. Some people are famished but they cannot feed. Others have to not only feed them but also decide for them what to eat. Some day try to be spoonfed, and you will know that it is not a wonderful experience.

Spoon-feeding is one of the things they teach nurses in their first year. To the person being fed, the amount of food on the spoon could be too little or too much. Also, the pace at which the food is being given will not align with the way the patient wants it, because the brain of the feeder is delivering the food at a pace that is not in consonance with the message that is being relayed by the brain of the patient to the salivary glands of the patient.

This could cause loss of appetite or mechanical eating—eating to fill the belly and not eating to enjoy the food. It is a thing of joy to eat what you want when you want it and at your own pace. This is because God has given you the power to feed. It is a gift of God. We should learn to thank God always in all situations. Here is a song for you:

> Some have food but cannot eat
> Some can eat but have no food
> I have food and I can eat
> Glory be to God on High
> Some can pooh but cannot pee
> Some can pee but cannot pooh
> I can pooh and I can pee
> Glory be to God on High

Insight is a great act that will give you a wonderful realization of what you are and have become through Him. You are a special selection. There is a chorus that says:

> Thank you Almighty Father among the multitudes you remember me.

Even when you think that things are not working out, be assured that He is working it out.

> In Him we also were made [God's] heritage (portion) and we obtained an inheritance; for we had been foreordained (chosen and appointed beforehand) in accordance with His purpose, Who works out everything in agreement with the counsel and design of His [own] will...
> (Ephesians 1:11, TAB)

I had a chat with a woman and she shared with me the story of a day when one of her daughters gave her a call from college. She recounted that the young lady was crying over the phone that she was tired of school (she was a fresh lady). She really missed her mom. After the young lady dropped the phone, the woman also started crying, and she cried all the way home from her office.

Why was she deeply filled with sorrow? Because she could not go and say hello to her daughter at her school. The daughter was schooling in another country but the mother had no legal papers that permitted her go to that country. She was an immigrant where she is. When this woman got home, she saw a letter in her mailbox inviting her for residency interview so that her immigration status could be regularized. In her words she remembered the lyrics from a song called

"AMEN"

by Bob Fitts:

> For every good thing
> God is doing within me
> That I cannot see
> A - men
> And to the healing virtue of Jesus
> That's flowing in me
> A - men
> For every hope that is still just a dream
> By trusting you Lord it becomes reality
> I stake my claim, seal it in faith
> I say amen
> Amen amen
> So be it Lord
> Your word endures
> I say amen
> Amen amen
> So be it Lord
> A - men

The song says "by trusting in you Lord it becomes reality." Trust is very important. Faith will allow you to take the first step but trust will ensure your steps do not falter. *While faith is the activity that activates the promise, trust is the posture that possesses the promise.*

Those who trust in the LORD are like Mount Zion, which cannot be shaken but endures forever. You may not be able to physically see it now but you have been predestined according to the plan of He who works out everything in conformity with the purpose of his will. You will be great, you shall be lifted, it shall be well with you, in Jesus' name. Amen.

This woman went for the interview and she was granted legal residency without frills. It seemed like a dream, too good to be true, when God turned around the captivity of Zion.

> For from Him and through Him and to Him are all things. [For all things originate with Him and come from Him; all things live through Him, and all things center in and tend to consummate and to end in Him.] To Him be glory forever! Amen (so be it). (Romans 11:36, TAB)

Everything evolved from him and you can only attain greatness through him so you have to look to him. If you are not a born again Christian, the devil will be the one inside you since there cannot be a vacuum. Let today be a turning point in your life. Invite him into your life so that he can live in you.

> Into my life, into my life
> Come into my life Lord Jesus
> Come in today, come in to stay
> Come into my life Lord Jesus

> For by him all things were created: things in heaven and on earth, visible and invisible, whether thrones or powers or

rulers or authorities; all things were created by him and for him. (Colossians 1:16, KJV)

For thou hast possessed my reins: thou hast covered me in my mother's womb. I will praise thee; for I am fearfully and wonderfully made: marvellous are thy works; and that my soul knoweth right well. (Psalm 139:13–14, KJV)

You are the righteousness of God through Christ Jesus. You have been purchased expensively. You are not cheap so do not sell yourself cheap. You are in right standing with God.

For God made Christ, who never sinned, to be the offering for our sin, so that we could be made right with God through Christ. (2 Corinthians 5:21, NLT)

The end to all your wanderings, the solution to all your problems lies inside; remember the one that is living in you called Emmanuel and the breath of life in you that has turned you into a living soul. Hear this story. There is a sports discussion forum that I sometimes log on to called "cybereagles." One day I logged in and I was constantly redirected to another web site. Do you know what had happened? A cracker had hijacked the site. He called himself "Dweevil." He registered himself on the forum because he technically owned the site the moment he disabled all the administrators.

A dialogue ensued with him during which he was asked what could be done to prevent such occurrences in future, and he gave an insight—a look inwards. He said the version of the software being used to run the site was very old, and there needs to be an upgrade.

The Word of God buttresses the above story.

Elisha said, "I wonder how I can be of help. Tell me, what do you have in your house?" "Nothing," she said. "Well, I do have a little oil. (2 Kings 4:2, MSG)

The woman in the above story had what would end her sorrow right in her house, but she did not know it. The way to your greatness is in your house. For us today as believers the oil represents the Holy Spirit, and we have Him in us. Sometimes all we need is an upgrade of our knowledge of the power of God.

When we have an insight concerning some situations plaguing us, we may discover that the only thing that we need to do is to transform our thought process. When an individual is looking for a job, he mails, emails or faxes his or her resume outside. This individual may eventually get the job and go outside to do the job. What has enabled him to get the job is what is inside and what will enable him to keep the job is also what is inside.

IQ (Intelligence Quotient) that is inside may get him the job, RQ (Relationship Quotient) that is also inside will enable him to keep the job. A man cannot give what he does not have. A snake will always spew venom. Whether IQ or RQ, it has been given. What do we have that has not been given? What do we possess that is not already His? A man cannot receive anything except it be given him from heaven. We have been loaded by the one who daily loads us with benefits.

Lack of insight causes husbands and wives to fight in the home over trivial issues. It would be nice if the couple would take time to consider just one good thing about their partner. Instead of looking outside for solutions in another man or woman or the lawyers chambers, look inside.

When a man is given an insight, it is the end of confusion in the life of that man. Fruitless effort comes to an end. God had to give Jeshua an insight into the cause of limitation, after which he was able to finish what he had started. He realized that he was like a burning stick snatched from the fire.

...is not this a brand plucked out of the fire?

(Zechariah 3:2, KJV)

An insight will ensure that you do not become a scaffold. A scaffold is only useful during the construction process, but it does not stay around to celebrate the beautiful structure that it has created. It is immediately packed away for use in the construction of another building, or placed in storage. A scaffold builds but does not inhabit. The Word of God already says concerning you that you shall not build and another inhabit. Sometimes all it takes is for you to simply say, "Satan the Lord rebuke you because I am a brand plucked out of fire." Nobody jokes with fire. Fire has wonderful attributes:

- It is confrontational–The fire of God will confront all your problems.
- It burns–All your problems shall be burnt away.
- It takes no captive–No problems (infirmities) shall reside in you again.
- It cannot be limited–Every limitation shall be burnt to ashes.

DESTINED FOR GREATNESS

Long before he laid down earth's foundations, he had us in mind, had settled on us as the focus of his love, to be made whole and holy by his love. Long, long ago he decided to adopt us into his family through Jesus Christ. (What pleasure he took in planning this!) He wanted us to enter into the celebration of his lavish gift-giving by the hand of his beloved Son. Because of the sacrifice of the Messiah, his blood poured out on the altar of the Cross, we're a free people—free of penalties and punishments chalked up by all our misdeeds. And not just barely free, either. Abundantly free!

He thought of everything, provided for everything we could possibly need, letting us in on the plans he took such delight in making. He set it all out before us in Christ, a long-range plan in which everything would be brought together and summed up in him, everything in deepest heaven, everything on planet earth. (Ephesians 1: 4–10, MSG)

Long before the first pronouncement came from the mouth of God to "let there be light," God already decided and preordained that he would create a species that would look like him. This species will be whole (nothing missing, nothing broken) and holy. God will bestow wonderful gifts on this species, and it shall be celebration galore.

He had it all planned out that this special species would be able to function in the highest heaven and on planet earth. They would be abundantly free, and glorious living would be their portion. The good news today is that God had it all designed. Your destiny is greatness.

Since God wants the best for his creation, he had to use the most awesome approach. To realize his plan, he decided to use two of the most powerful offices in the world—kings and priests. While a king's domain and power is terrestrial, that of a priest is predominantly celestial. A king can be likened to the president or prime minister of a nation. A king has the ability to put into effect natural laws, constitutions, or in some cases, decrees. A priest, on the other hand, has the ability to put into effect spiritual laws and also provides the atmosphere for natural laws to operate.

The king and the priest have their limitations because they are separate entities. Imagine one man holding the same office and having the power associated with the offices. He can connect and communicate with God (priest), and he can also function and be fruitful on earth (king).

David functioned as a king and a priest. Jesus came to perfect the plan and he excelled as a king and a priest. As children of God, you have the DNA or gene of Jesus flowing in you. Long before we first heard of Christ and got our hopes up, he had his eye on us, had designs on us for *glorious living.*

In heavenly matters, a priest excels, while in earthly matters a king excels. In many cases you see priests or men of God running to kings for favour (e.g. Isaiah to Uzziah). Kings also run to priests (e.g. kings to Elisha). The most appalling situation to God is when a priest will run to an earthly king. God decided to correct the situation.

> All right then, the Lord himself will choose the sign. Look! The virgin will conceive a child! She will give birth to a son and will call him Immanuel—God is with us.
> (Isaiah 7:14, NLT)

> For a child has been born—for us! the gift of a son—for us! He'll take over the running of the world. His names will be: Amazing Counselor, Strong God, Eternal Father, Prince of Wholeness. (Isaiah 9:6, MSG)

The DNA of a king and a priest was in His blood. In giving your life to Him, His blood is also flowing in your veins.

"Therefore if any man be in Christ he is a new creature:old things are passed away;behold, all things are become new." (2 Corinthians 5:17, KJV), i.e. you have a different genotype. The blood of Jesus is flowing in your veins. Besides all the antigens and antibodies in the blood are royalty (kingship) and priesthood. This is why the Word of God calls you king and priests unto Him.

> And hath made us kings and priests unto God and his Father; to him be glory and dominion for ever and ever. Amen. (Revelations 1:6, KJV)

Apostle Peter also said "you are a royal priesthood," i.e. *you can now commune with heaven, convey the communication to the earth, and conquer the land.* A plane that takes off from an airport already knows where it is going to land; not only that, but the Estimated Time of Arrival (ETA) is also known. As children of God, our destination is glorious living. While some know this fact, most do not know the ETA. The ETA is now. It has already been determined. God said by the mouth of the prophet Isaiah that, "I will do a new thing and now it shall spring forth," the psalmist said, "now is the time to favor Zion, the set time has come."

There was a man that functioned in this capacity even before Christ that we could look at as a case study. David made a decision to tackle Goliath and some of the challenges he faced are below. He was:

ISOLATED

Preparatory to facing Goliath, David was equipped with the wrong attire. The attire, though later discarded, was a form of encouragement by King Saul. When the real battle started, David was alone on the battlefield with Goliath. No matter the encouragement that you receive, you still have to fight your battles. The pugilist will have a trainer, a doctor, even a sparring partner preparatory to the real bout. On the day of the bout, there will be lots of people in the arena cheering and jeering but when the bell sounds, he is alone with the adversary.

Isolation, though at times dreadful, also has its advantages. A season of preparation requires a season of separation. If you are isolated now, regard it as a time of preparation. There is a time to celebrate and also a time to prepare. When Jacob was going to face Esau, he had to separate himself from his family and attendants. He was left alone to wrestle with God at Peniel. After the wrestling bout, he was given a new name, and the problem

This is why we were separated from our entire family since the launch of 2020 & Sept 15, 2020 he came to pray about became solved because when he finally met Esau, instead of a fight, it was favor galore. *Isolation births illumination.*

IMPROPERLY ARMED

David was attired in garments and implements that he had not proved. He settled on seven smooth stones. The smoothness of the stones shows they have been tested at the riverbed because the water had washed over them and they did not crack. Everything that will not make them go as directed had been eroded.

Do you think you are improperly attired right now? In the challenges of life, the Rock will always work. The Rock is none other than Jesus, or the Word of God. He is not slack concerning His promises. He is the Rock of offence and the Rock of ages. *To the ordinary eye, when David went to face Goliath without any spear, helmet, sword or shield, he was improperly armed, not knowing that he was immortally armed.* The immortal, invisible and only wise God that specializes in equipping the called is still on the throne. You have all it takes to be the person He wants you to be.

IMMATURE

This simply means David was a small boy. He was not ready for the challenge he undertook. A deep revelation is that he is not too big for God to carry. A wonderful attribute of God is that He loves to carry His children. People that are too big for God cannot be carried by God. A good attribute of children is that they believe without doubting whatever their parents say. When the Word of God says He will go before you to make every crooked way straight and every bent way smooth, you have to believe Him.

When God says you will not need to fight in this battle but the battle is His, you need to hold fast unto His word. David simply believed the Word of God. *"Say ye to the righteous it shall be well with him."* (Isaiah 3:10, KJV)

Despite the fact that God had earmarked us for greatness, we can decide to move from the path of greatness. If you are on the path of greatness you will know as the attributes are outlined below.

A GOOD CUSTODIAN

God is always looking for those that will keep the little they have at the moment. David was a good custodian. To be a good custodian implies that you value what you have. It also means to tend, watch or keep.

> And Samuel said to Jesse, "Are all the young men here?" Then he said, "There remains yet the youngest, and there he is, keeping the sheep. (1 Samuel 16:11, NKJV)

When he was sent on an errand by Jesse to see how his brothers were doing at the warfront, he did something wonderful; he left the sheep with somebody else. Others would have locked them in a grazing ground and left them at the mercy of lions and bears.

> "So David rose early in the morning, left the sheep with a keeper..." (1 Samuel 17:20, NKJV)

When he got to the battle front, he did not forget to keep those things that his father gave to him.

> And David left his supplies in the hand of the supply keeper, ran to the army, and came and greeted his brothers.
> (1 Samuel 17:22, NKJV)

At the battlefront, his brother contended against his ability to keep.

> But when David's oldest brother, Eliab, heard David talking to the men, he was angry. "What are you doing around here anyway?" he demanded. "What about those few sheep you're supposed to be taking care of? (1 Samuel 17:28, NLT)

The ability to keep is present in the King of Kings and Lord of Lords. The psalmist said, *"The* LORD *is thy keeper: the* LORD *is thy shade upon thy right hand"*(Psalm 121:5, KJV*)*.

When Saul also contended with David's ability to go to war against Goliath David said, "I am a keeper." He had the word "keeper" in his resume.

> "And David said unto Saul, Thy servant kept his father's sheep, and there came a lion, and a bear, and took a lamb out of the flock:"(1 Samuel 17:34, KJV)

One attribute that the devil will always contend with is your ability to keep whatever the Lord gives to you. This is something that he will always bring to the remembrance of Jehovah, that whatever He gives you, you will not be able to keep. The servant with the one talent thought he knew the best way to keep whatever is entrusted to him when he dug a hole and hid the talent.

The prodigal son failed in his ability to keep the inheritance. He spent everything on wild living. When Jesus was about to leave this terra firma in the flesh, He gave an account of His stewardship. He said all that the Father gave to Him He has kept except the son of perdition.

KNOWS HIS LIMIT

Something noteworthy that a man destined for greatness

recognizes is that he has limits. This is born out of the recognition that anything that he is ever going to achieve will be dependent on God.

Paul can plant and Apollos water, but it is only God that gives the increase. The horse may be prepared against the day of battle but safety is of the Lord. It is not of him that wills nor of him that runs but of the Lord that shows mercy. Except the Lord build the house, they labor in vain that build it.

> I returned, and saw under the sun, that the race is not to the
> swift, nor the battle to the strong, neither yet bread to the
> wise, nor yet riches to men of understanding, nor yet favor
> to men of skill; but time and chance happeneth to them all.
> (Ecclesiastes 9:1, KJV)

There is a difference between faith and folly. There is the story of a man in a university in Nigeria that wanted to be a modern day Daniel. He jumped into the lion's den, and he started praying and reciting scriptures. Alas, he became a sumptuous meal for the lions. At the time this happened (I attended the university), I was not a Christian and this was further proof that I should not have anything to do with Christians, that they are fools. I thank God for his mercies for allowing me to see the light and for bringing me out of the miry clay.

> While faith has its source in the Savior, folly is rooted in self.
> It seeks to glorify man and not God. A step of faith is mostly
> born out of need, while folly is due to inordinate ambition.

> David said moreover, The LORD that delivered me out of
> the paw of the lion, and out of the paw of the bear, he will
> deliver me out of the hand of this Philistine. And Saul said
> unto David, Go, and the LORD be with thee.
> (1 Samuel 17:37, KJV)

Because a man destined for greatness knows his limit:

HE DOES NOT DECEIVE HIMSELF

> And David girded his sword over his armor. Then he tried to go, but could not, for he was not used to it. And David said to Saul, I cannot go with these, for I am not used to them. And David took them off. (1 Samuel 17:39, **TAB**)

A man destined for greatness does not get entangled in frivolities.

> And David said, What have I done now? Was it not a harmless question? And David turned away from Eliab to another and he asked the same question, and again the men gave him the same answer. (1 Samuel 17:29–30, **TAB**)

Apostle Paul, in his letter to Timothy, mentioned that no one serving as a soldier gets involved in civilian affairs because he wants to please his commanding officer, and an athlete involved in a competition does not receive the victor's medal unless he competes according to the laid down rules. David had two wonderful opportunities to end the reign of Saul, but he realized that it is better for God to enthrone him than he doing it by himself. His men whispered to him that this is what the Lord is talking about when He said He will give David's enemies to him, but David declined to take the offer.

> David's men whispered to him, "Can you believe it? This is the day God was talking about when he said, 'I'll put your enemy in your hands. You can do whatever you want with him.'" Quiet as a cat, David crept up and cut off a piece of Saul's royal robe. Immediately, he felt guilty. He said to his men, "God forbid that I should have done this to my mas-

ter, God's anointed, that I should so much as raise a finger against him. He's God's anointed!
(1 Samuel 24:4–6, MSG)

Abishai said, "This is the moment! God has put your enemy in your grasp. Let me nail him to the ground with his spear. One hit will do it, believe me; I won't need a second!" But David said to Abishai, "Don't you dare hurt him! Who could lay a hand on God's anointed and even think of getting away with it? (1 Samuel 26:8–9, MSG)

God is not a liar. Whatever height of glory that He has purposed for you will definitely be attained. Make sure you are truthful. Do not be a traitor or conspirator.

NUGGETS

- Insight is a deep perception of a situation.
- For any man or family that desires growth, there has to be a constant inward looking (insight).
- Growth begins from the source.
- An inward look or insight will reveal that He who is inside is the Almighty God.
- Things that God can do:
- God has the power to eliminate your enemies.
- God has the power to calm every calamity.
- God has the power to exalt every exiled.
- God has the power to feed the famished. Therefore, only trust in Him.
- While faith is the activity that activates the promise, trust is the posture that possesses the promise.
- An insight will ensure that you do not become a scaffold (only useful to build, but does not enjoy what has been built).
- No matter the encouragement that you receive, you still have to fight your own battles.
- A season of preparation requires a season of separation.
- Remember that you are destined for greatness. A man destined for greatness must:
- Be a good custodian.
- Know his limit
- Realize that everything that he can ever be is dependent upon the grace of God.
- Not get entangled in frivolities.

PRAYER POINTS

- Father, the insight that will enable me grow, until I become very great, give unto me, in Jesus' mighty name.
- Lord, destroy completely every seed of desolation in my life and in all that concerns me. Let there be progress and excellence in all that pertains to me.
- Oh Lord, everything in me that wants to destroy me, annihilate completely, in Jesus' name.
- The treasures that have been deposited in me, spring forth, in Jesus' name.
- Father, even as Isaac grew, I will grow. I will expand, increase, become more evident and develop, in Jesus' name. Amen.
- Lord God, pummel every nemesis of my life into submission, be it sickness, anger, lies, frivolous living, debt, discouragement, defeat, fear. Destroy every enemy of my greatness, in Jesus' name.
- Jesus, in every way I have been exiled from my greatness, exalt me into your position of honor for my life.
- Father, I know I have been designed for glorious living, to show forth your light and glory; let it start in my life now, in Jesus' name.
- Heavenly Father, your time to favor me has come; let it start now, in Jesus' name.
- Father, help me to be a good custodian of what you have given me, and help me know my limits and avoid frivolities, in Jesus' name.

INSULT

Slander cannot destroy the man... when the flood recedes, the rock is there.

-Chinese Proverb

He accumulated flocks and herds and many, many servants, so much so that the Philistines began to envy him. They got back at him by throwing dirt and debris into all the wells that his father's servants had dug back in the days of his father Abraham, clogging up all the wells."
(Genesis 26: 14–15, MSG)

A pillar that has accelerated or hastened the attainment of great men's destinies is insult. Isaac, because he was progressing, became envied. With envy came maltreatment, spite, resentment and hostility. It is an unfriendly disposition. He was later thrown out of the city but he took everything in good stride. He turned the pain to gain, the insult to increase.

Every man or woman needs insult or ill will so that there can be a constant alertness. When men are constantly singing your praise, you lose sight of the objective. Insult, if properly channelled, can be a fertilizer towards greatness. You need challenges to take you to the next dimension in kingdom excellence. Envy, insult or ill will is what is called PHD (Pull Him/Her Down). If you give in to certain situations, they will drag you down.

Joseph suffered from constant ridicule by his brothers. They had nothing good to say about him. He was hated. To compound his problem, he had a picture of a better future. He was not shy to let everyone know where God was taking him. He thought he had blood brothers but he had forgotten that a man's greatest enemy are members of his own household.

He was sent by his father to see how his brothers were doing instead of his brothers reciprocating this kind gesture with love, he was first thrown into a pit then sold into slavery. His predicament did not end there. The wife of his master lied against him and got him thrown into jail.

With all that Joseph faced, many would have given up on life. Some would take to drugs or commit suicide but in the dungeon, Joseph was still excelling. The keeper of the prison entrusted other prisoners into his care.

His dreams eventually came to pass and he rose to become the next in command to the king of Egypt. While in the dungeon he did not forget his dream and he eventually wore the diadem. When he met his brothers after a while, he was able to tell them that what they did was an activator for his destiny.

> "But as for you, ye thought evil against me; but God meant it unto good, to bring to pass, as it is this day, to save much people alive."(Genesis 50:20, KJV)

In life it is not so much what we encounter, but how we handle what we encounter. I have heard the story of a man that won a lot of money in lottery but today the man is a wreck. All the money had been squandered and he now lives in a dilapidated building. There is a story about what happened to Christians in Meulaboh, Indonesia, prior to the tsunami. It was allegedly written by the pastor of Calvary Life Fellowship. There has been different opinions about this story. The story is below:

> "On December 26th, 2004 the whole world heard about a tragedy in Asia, Tsunami. Pastor Bill Hekman of Calvary Life Fellowship in Indonesia has this to say about a certain event that

preceeded the outburst of the Tsunami. We know that 80% of the town of Meulaboh in Aceh, Indonesia was destroyed by the Tsunami waves and 80% of the people also died. This is one of the towns that was hit the hardest. But there is a fantastic testimony from Meulaboh. In that town are about 400 Christians.

They wanted to celebrate Christmas on December 25th but were not allowed to do so by the Muslims of Meulaboh. They were told if they wanted to celebrate Christmas they needed to go outside the city of Meulaboh on a high hill and there celebrate Christmas. Because the Christians desired to celebrate Christmas the 400 believers left the city on December 25th and after they celebrated Christmas they stayed overnight on the hill.

As we all know, on the morning of December 26 there was the earthquake followed by the Tsunami waves destroying most of the city of Meulaboh and thousands were killed. The 400 believers were on the mountain and were all saved from destruction. Now the Muslims of Meulaboh are saying that the God of the Christians punished us for forbidding the Christians from celebrating Christmas in the city.

Others are questioning why so many Muslims died while not even one of the Christians died there. Had the Christians insisted on their rights to celebrate Christmas in the city, they would have all died. But because they humbled themselves and followed the advice of the Muslims, they all were spared destruction and can now testify of God's marvelous protection. This is a testimony of the grace of God and the fact that as believers we have no rights in the world. Our right is to come before God and commit our lives to Him. Our right is kneeling down before the Lord almighty and committing our ways to Him. He is our Father and is very capable to care for His children. Praise the Name of the Lord."

The church web site also says: "We have confirmed the story via phone and email with Bill Hekman and through an Indonesian pastor who has heard the story from several persons with first-hand knowledge, as follows:

> This is the account from the believers in Meulaboh. The 400 believers involved are from the Roman Catholic Church, GPIB Church and HKPB Church. They had requested permission from the District Leader (Camat), Police (POLRES) and DANDIM (Army) to celebrate Christmas in Meulaboh. They were told that since Meulaboh is under Sharia Islamic law it would be better to go somewhere where there are no Moslems. So the believers left the morning of Dec. 25th and walked about 5 kms. to a hill area. They were accompanied by some members of the Marine Corps who were also Christians. They celebrated Christmas the afternoon of Dec. 25th and stayed there for the night at a "Retreat." They had brought food, etc. to camp there for the night. The tsunami took place the morning of the 26th of Dec. These believers are now refugees living in Aceh Jaya."

No matter your stance about this story, what I want to bring to your attention from it is the way to handle perceived insults. The Christians in Meulaboh could have said, "What an insult; we have as much right as the Muslims in this city." Little did they know that everything is fitting into a divine plan. When unbearable insults are thrown at you, why don't you take it to God in prayer?

> "Not only that—count yourselves blessed every time people put you down or throw you out or speak lies about you to discredit me. What it means is that the truth is too close for comfort and they are uncomfortable. You can be glad when that happens—give a cheer, even!-for though they don't like it, I do! And all heaven applauds. And know that you are in good company." (Matthew 5:11–12, MSG)

HOW TO REACT TO INSULTS

Reflect, not Reflex

Our human subconscious wants to defend or say something back when insults are thrown our way. In some other cases we want to really prove that the other person or party does not know anything. We display a knee jerk reaction or come shooting from the hips with guns blazing, firing from all cylinders. Instead of a reflex reaction, we need to reflect. Jesus Christ taught on persecution and when he was ridiculed, he practiced what he preached.

Phillip, one of the disciples of Jesus, found a man called Nathanael and told him about Jesus. The response of Nathanael was an insult to the origin of Jesus. "Can any good thing come out of Nazareth. Jesus heard this and he did not feel "dissed," instead he complimented Nathanael.

> And Nathanael said unto him, Can there any good thing come out of Nazareth? Philip saith unto him, Come and see. Jesus saw Nathanael coming to him, and saith of him, Behold an Israelite indeed, in whom is no guile!
> (John 1:46–47, KJV)

Phillip's response must also be noted. He simply said, "come and see." The taste of the pudding is in the eating. Insult or ill will may try to shift your focus but you must not give in. Envy is the tribute that mediocrity pays to excellence.

> You can't hold a man down without staying down with him
> - Booker T. Washington

The writer or coiner of words did not make a mistake with a word called "backbite." There is nothing like "frontbite" in the English language. Those that backbite will always be at the back. The people that were envying Isaac were jealous of his achievement. Isaac did not stoop to their level; he simply moved on and dug more wells. Gospel artist Ron Kenoly, in one of his songs, said, "if you catch hell don't hold it, if you are going through hell don't stop, just go ahead." This song advises on the stance to take when insult is heaped your way.

Compare the response of Jesus to that of a powerful king. He became a king at the age of sixteen. He reigned for 52 years. The Word of God says better is the end of a thing than the beginning thereof. One day he usurped the role of a priest and went into the temple to burn incense that is contrary to the levitical laws. The priest by the name Azariah corrected him.

> It is not right for you, Uzziah, to burn incense to the LORD. That is for the priests, the descendants of Aaron, who have been consecrated to burn incense. Leave the sanctuary, for you have been unfaithful; and you will not be honored by the LORD God. (2Chronicles 26:18, NIV)

Instead of listening, King Uzziah lashed out; instead of him reflecting on the love, mercy and grace of God that allowed him to succeed his father and sustained him while on the throne, he reacted by flexing his kingly muscles.

> Uzziah was furious and refused to set down the incense burner he was holding. But as he was standing there with the priests before the incense altar in the LORD's Temple, leprosy suddenly broke out on his forehead.
> (2 Chronicles 26:19, NLT)

Instead of living the rest of his years in a palace, he died in a leper colony, all because he could not pause to reflect.

WEEDS AMONG WHEAT

Insults or ill will are nothing but weeds among wheat. Jesus once told a parable of a farmer who planted good seed of wheat in his field. At night while everyone was sleeping, his enemies came and planted weeds among the wheat. When the crops started growing into grains, the weeds also grew.

His servants reported their observations to him and he quickly identified the cause–an enemy has done this. The servants furthermore inquired concerning what to do with the weeds, and he replied, "let the weeds grow so that we do not pull out the good grains while trying to pull out the weeds." When the time of harvest comes, we will be able to pull out the weeds and burn them. The fruit will make the weeds and the wheat distinct. There are a couple of deep revelations in this story.

The man did not panic. He did not fret himself because of evildoers. He furthermore identified the cause and in effect the reason for the problem. An enemy had done this. An enemy has only one aim—to steal, kill and destroy. To steal your joy, kill your dream, and destroy your harvest. The man did not allow any of this to happen.

If he had followed the advice of the servants, his harvest would have been either reduced (some of the wheat grains would have been pulled out) or retarded (some of the wheat grains would have been rendered unhealthy).

When your approach to insult or ill will is negative, you are working against your harvest to either retard or reduce it. You will not be able to hold onto the promises of God. Doubt will begin to creep in. Your situation could become just what Satan said to Eve; "did God indeed say that?" If you believe the lie of Satan, with your own hand you begin to pull out the good seed.

Another thing that must be mentioned in this story is that the man was sure of what he planted. He was sure that it was a good seed. This informed the decision to let it grow. He was convinced that it would grow. The good word of the Lord concerning your life will surely grow in Jesus' name.

A SUMMARY OF LESSONS
FROM THE STORY:

- Plant good seed—Galatians 6:10, 1Timothy 6:18, Hebrews 13:16
- Have a field—Genesis 2:15, Proverbs 12:24, Deuteronomy 28:3
- There is a Turning Point—Genesis 32:24–30
- There is a time for rest—Ecclesiastes 3:1, Genesis 2:2, Isaiah 30:15
- There is an enemy—1Peter 5:8, John 10:10, Revelation 12:10
- The enemy can also plant—1Chronicles 21:1, Genesis 4:7,
- The seed of the enemy is bad—Genesis 3:6–7, Proverbs 20:17
- Both the good and the bad will grow—Genesis 4:1–9
- Everything good comes with a price—2Corinthians 4:8–10, Philippians 4:12
- When there is growth, people will notice—Nehem. 6:1, 1Chron.14:1, 1Kings 10:1
- People also know what you have planted—Hebrews 12:1
- There is respect for the good—John 14:1–3, Matthew 25:14–23
- The growth of the weeds is always fast—Ecclesiastes 8:11–13
- Know the source of your predicament—2Kings 2:19–21, Jonah 1:7
- People will give counsel—1Samuel 24:4, 1Samuel 26:8, 2Samuel 13:3
- Know the counsel to take or ignore—2 Samuel 13:6, 1Kings 12:8

- It is always easy to pull out the weed—Luke 17:34–36, Matthew 13:6
- Do everything to protect the good seed—Proverbs 4:23, 1Peter 1:23
- The wheat can be hurt—1Kings 19:4
- Wheat and weeds have a limited life span—Hebrews 9:27, Ecc. 3:2, 2Pet. 1:14
- The wheat and weeds both have a destination—John 14:1–3, Revelation 21:8
- Have a plan—1Corinthians 9:26, Jeremiah 29:11

HOPEFUL, NOT HOPELESS

The Word of God says hope does not bring about shame. When the wind of ill will blows your way, do not allow it to blow away your hope. For surely there is a hereafter. After the rainfall there is sunshine, after darkness there is light, and after night there is morning.

Another name for God is hope. The Word of God says that "Abraham against hope, believed in hope." Job was a man that was insulted and ridiculed by friends because they could not fathom how a man who claimed to love God could experience such mind-boggling catastrophes in a matter of hours. He lost his children and his property. To compound his misery, he was afflicted by a strange illness, and his wife deserted him.

The first words that came out of the mouth of his supposed friends that came to comfort him were these:

> Stop and think! Does the innocent person perish? When has the upright person been destroyed? My experience shows that those who plant trouble and cultivate evil will harvest the same. (Job 4:7–8, MSG)

— Trudeau
- Faul - Ci
- WEF & Bill Gates a.k.a - Lucifers minions
- Can be anyone...

In effect, these friends were saying that whatever has befallen him must be due to his own handiwork. He is being punished for his misdeeds. They even taunted him that he should call on God now, and see if God will answer. In all these, Job did not sin against the Almighty God.

Job told his friends, "To him that is afflicted pity should be shown from his friends." Job held unto a glorious hope, for Christ in you is the hope of Glory. Sometimes we need to glory in tribulations, for it brings about patience, and patience brings about hope. Hopelessness takes away faith from us, and without faith it is impossible to please God. We have access into his grace by faith.

The Lord is a sun and shield and he will give grace and glory no good thing will he withhold from them that walk uprightly. When you are hopeless, you are not walking uprightly. In all the trials and tribulations of Job he was able to confess:

> But as for me, I know that my Redeemer lives, and that he will stand upon the earth at last. And after my body has decayed, yet in my body I will see God! I will see him for myself. Yes, I will see him with my own eyes. I am overwhelmed at the thought! (Job 19:25–27, NLT)

WISDOM, NOT WORRY

Jacob was a man of wisdom. Due to his cunning, he had to leave his parents for the house of his uncle. On getting there, he fell in love with one of his uncle's daughters, Rachel, and he told his uncle Laban that he wanted to marry her. The bride price was seven years of servitude. He took it in good stride. After serving for the seven years, he was given another girl, Leah, instead of Rachel.

When Jacob discovered this, he insisted on having Rachel. This meant he had to serve for another seven years, and Jacob complied without worrying. One of the things that wisdom gives is peace because you know what the others do not know.

Afterwards, the same Laban asked Jacob to continue to work on his farm for a fee to be named by Jacob. Jacob gave a ridiculous fee that Laban was pleased with because it seemed devoid of wisdom.

> [Laban] said, What shall I give you? And Jacob said, You shall not give me anything, if you will do this one thing for me [of which I am about to tell you], and I will again feed and take care of your flock. Let me pass through all your flock today, removing from it every speckled and spotted animal and every black one among the sheep, and the spotted and speckled among the goats; and such shall be my wages. (Genesis 30:31–3, TAB)

Historians have said that in the East in those days, the sheep were almost uniformly white. The black, brown and spotted animals of any kind were rare. For Jacob to select the rare animals as his wage really pleased Laban.

> When you ask a wise man to make a selection, and he does not choose the obvious, you have to beware
> - Pastor E.A. Adeboye

Instead of worrying, let us ask for wisdom. The Word of God says that wisdom is the principal thing and if anybody lacks wisdom, he should ask. Wisdom gives an ornament of grace and a crown of glory. When I was in the university, we had different kinds of courses; some were electives while others were compulsory. The compulsory courses were the "principal" ones. The marks that you get in the principal ones will determine your ultimate grade at the time of graduation. You can decide that you do not want to do the electives but you do not have such liberty when it comes to the compulsory courses. God is saying wisdom is compulsory.

> Wisdom is as good as an inheritance, yes, more excellent it is for those [the living] who see the sun. For wisdom is a defense even as money is a defense, but the excellency of knowledge is that wisdom shields and preserves the life of him who has it. (Ecclesiastes 7:11–12, TAB)

Back to the story of Jacob and Laban. At the time of conception, the animals brought forth progeny that were spotted and speckled. Jacob increased exceedingly by relying on the wisdom of God. Situations that come our way that cause us to worry can be called solid food. It is not for babes, but for those that will be able to eat and digest. Little children can only eat milk when born but with time they are able to eat solid food. When a little child is hungry, to seek attention he must cry or, in some cases, wail. Such is not expected from adults. You go and prepare your food or ask. You do what is right.

> Solid food is for those who are mature, who have trained themselves to recognize the difference between right and wrong and then do what is right. (Hebrews 5:14, NLT)

I once read the story of a man that walked into a bank to take a loan of about $5,000.00 to go on a vacation for two weeks. The loan officer requested collateral for such a loan, and the man said he would use his $80,000.00 BMW as collateral. The loan was granted speedily and the deal signed, sealed and delivered. The bank took possession of the car and secured it. The bank employees scorned the man after he left at such stupidity.

When the redemption date came, the man walked into the bank, paid off the loan, principal and interest that amounted to less than $20.00. The loan officer then asked why he did such a thing, and he said he had no place to pack the car for the period of his vacation. He retorted "Where else can you pack a car of such value for less than $20.00 and still expect to meet it safe upon arrival except a bank?"

Wisdom is of more value than foolishness...
(Ecclesiastes 2:13, NLT)

ALERT NOT ALOOF

Many people have been derailed on the path to greatness due to comfort. This is a false sense of security.

Woe to those who are at ease in Zion... (Amos 6:1, TAB)

King David had a false sense of security and it caused confusion in his kingdom. When Kings led the troops to war, David stayed back in Jerusalem, and on a particular evening he saw a lady that was having her bath. He lusted after the woman, and had her brought to the palace. He had an affair with the woman, and it resulted in pregnancy.

This woman was the wife of one of the soldiers that went to war. For David to cover his tracks, he had to commit murder. Sin will take you further than you imagine. All these happened because he became too comfortable.

There is nothing wrong in being comfortable, but what is wrong is neglecting to do what you ought to do. Sometimes insults or ill will come our way because God wants to keep us alert. I once heard a story from the General Overseer of the Redeemed Christian Church of God, Pastor E.A. Adeboye, about an event on an airplane.

The plane went through turbulence to the extent that everybody started panicking and thinking that it was the end. At first he said he did not really take note but when the turbulence persisted and worsened, he paused to pray. He then thanked God for how He has been with Him and asked Him, "Is it time for me to come home?" He said God responded that He just wanted to talk to him and the only way to get his attention was through the turbulence. This man was not slothful, but God wanted to spend more time with him. Trials sometimes come our way not because we are laid back, but because God wants us to be on our toes. He wants our wavelength to always be at a frequency that is tuned to Him.

ADVANCE IN ADVERSITY

We do not know ourselves until we encounter adversity. Our maturity is measured by how we manage what we do not like, or do not expect. Jabez was a man whose own mother gave the name sorrow. This implies that anytime his mother sees him, she begins to weep. Jabez was more honorable and distinguished than his brothers; still, the mother named him sorrow.

Jabez was a carrier of sorrow. Anywhere he went, sorrow followed him. He would be faced with constant taunting and ridicule. No matter how distinguished he was, there was still a big "but" in his life. Instead of staying in the miry clay, he decided to advance. No mention was made of his father. He could hide under the guise that, "it is because my mother is a single mother, or I have an absentee father, or I am from a poor family."

Jabez called on the God of heaven. Unto him that answers prayer shall all flesh come. He said, "God bless me indeed." "Indeed" is a word used to show the intensity of a statement. He wanted God to bless him beyond any doubt. It is the blessing of God that makes rich, and He adds no sorrow to it. Jabez realized that if he became blessed by the God of heaven, an end would come to insult in his life.

And Jabez was more honourable than his brethren: and his mother called his name Jabez, saying, Because I bare him with sorrow. And Jabez called on the God of Israel, saying, Oh that thou wouldest bless me indeed, and enlarge my coast, and that thine hand might be with me, and that thou wouldest keep me from evil, that it may not grieve me! And God granted him that which he requested."

(I Chronicles 4:9–10, KJV)

Adversity is a hurdle that we always have to cross in life. Adversity has a way of proving our love for God. A time of adversity is a period to adhere to God so that he can advance us. It is a test of our ability to endure.

THE LAW OF FLOW AND OVERFLOW

For just as the sufferings of Christ flow over into our lives, so also through Christ our comfort overflows.

(2 Corinthians 1:5, NIV)

Paul said if we allow the sufferings of Christ to flow into our lives, the same Christ would ensure, validate, certify and, without fail, bring about an overflow of comfort. As Christians (those that manifest the qualities and adhere to the teachings of Jesus), we speak and quote the Word of God; for example: *"So shall my word be that goeth forth out of my mouth: it shall not return unto me void, but it shall accomplish that which I please, and it shall prosper in the thing whereto I sent it."*(Isaiah 55:11, KJV)

God is not a man, that He should lie. He is not a human, that He should change His mind. Has He ever spoken and failed to act? Has He ever promised and not carried it through? (Numbers 23:19, NLT)

But we sometimes fail in carrying out His simple instructions (laws) for example:

And it shall come to pass, if thou shalt hearken diligently unto the voice of the LORD thy God, to observe and to do all His commandments which I command thee this day, that the LORD thy God will set thee on high above all nations of the earth: (Deuteronomy 28:1, KJV)

Consider it a sheer gift, friends, when tests and challenges come at you from all sides. (James 1:2, MSG)

Looking at the two verses of scripture in Deuteronomy and James, we have been asked not only to observe but also to do. This means carrying out the injunctions from the Lord. One of the injunctions can be seen in the book of James which says to consider it a sheer gift when tests and challenges comes our way. In effect, insults should be considered a gift, adversities should be considered a gift, trials and tribulations should be considered a gift. When we understand this, we will be able to apply it to the Word of God that says, the gift of a man makes room for him. Trials have made a way for lots of people because the inherent gift in them has shown up in the face of adversity. A gift is a precious stone in the eyes of him that has it. Wherever it turns it prospers. The trial you are facing has an ultimate end, which is triumph.

Though suffering may flow in, let joy unspeakable overflow. "To them God has chosen to make known among the Gentiles the glorious riches of this mystery, which is Christ in you, the hope of glory."(Colossians 1:27, NIV)

Insults and ill will, though malicious and pernicious, are loose thoughts; emotions and unguarded impulses meant to derail or deride us. They are meant to manipulate us into doing what will keep us from attaining our destiny. What we need to do is make sure we fit them into the structure of the life shaped by Christ.

The tools of our trade aren't for marketing or manipulation, but they are for demolishing that entire massively corrupt culture. We use our powerful God-tools for smashing warped philosophies, tearing down barriers erected against the truth of God, fitting every loose thought and emotion and impulse into the structure of life shaped by Christ. Our tools are ready at hand for clearing the ground of every obstruction and building lives of obedience into maturity. (2 Corinthians 10: 4–6, MSG) *This is what Gods Kingdom Army is about.*

For though we walk in the flesh, we do not war after the flesh: (For the weapons of our warfare are not carnal, but mighty through God to the pulling down of strong holds;) (2 Corinthians 10:3–4, KJV)

Enemy's defeat

The Christian walk or race is that of warfare. Make no mistake about it. If it was not so, God would not have said put on the whole armor of God. *"Put on the whole armour of God, that ye may be able to stand against the wiles of the devil"* (Ephesians 6:11, KJV) neither would he have mentioned endure hardness like a good soldier

Thou therefore endure hardness, as a good soldier of Jesus Christ. No man that warreth entangleth himself with the affairs of this life; that he may please him who hath chosen him to be a soldier. (2 Timothy 2:3–4, KJV)

It is imperative to know how to fight this fight Paul said, *"I do not fight as one beating the air"* (1 Corinthians 9:26, KJV) (i.e. I use my energy on what is right, not chasing shadows). It is because we are beating the air that we say, like Gideon, *"if God is for us why are all these things befalling us"* (Judges 6:13). He was threshing wheat in a wine press.

For any effective warfare, there has to be weapon(s): an instrument of attack or defense in combat. The instrument is in us but it is only developed and sharpened over time as we grow in the Lord (e.g. a smith fashioning an instrument or sharpening it when it becomes crude).

A peculiarity of this weapon or the determinants of the effectiveness of this weapon are carnality and God. The Word of God says the weapon is not carnal but mighty through God (i.e. if the weapon is carnal it is brittle, but if it is spirit-filled it is potent). No matter the weapon that any Christian has, it can only be either mighty through God or useless through carnality. Note the word *through* God. Carnality is enmity with God.

Because the carnal mind is enmity against God: for it is not subject to the law of God, neither indeed can be. (Romans 8:7, KJV) This simply implies that God examines every weapon in warfare. After the thorough inspection he then decides whether the weapon can be made mighty, or only fit for the trash bin. When a weapon is examined and it passes the inspection, it goes through a process of "mightiness" by divine conversion. This is the reason why a prayer is said in the corner of your room and the effect is seen thousands of kilometers away.

For God to examine the weapon, he will also need to scrutinize the owner of the weapon.

> For as many as are led by the Spirit of God, they are the sons of God. For ye have not received the spirit of bondage again to fear; but ye have received the Spirit of adoption, whereby we cry, Abba, Father. The Spirit itself beareth witness with our spirit, that we are the children of God: (Romans 8:14–16, KJV)

A lot of Christians coat their weapon in carnality and expect results. If carnality is the backbone of warfare, it will ultimately be the bane of any victory achieved. Carnality cannot sustain or give longevity to anything.

I have seen wicked people buried with honor. How strange that they were the very ones who frequented the Temple and are praised in the very city where they committed their crimes! When a crime is not punished, people feel it is safe to do wrong. But even though a person sins a hundred times and still lives a long time, I know that those who fear God will be better off. The wicked will never live long, good lives, for they do not fear God. Their days will never grow long like the evening shadows. (Ecclesiastes 8:10–13, NLT)

Many Christians fall into the trap of envying, and subsequently comparing themselves to unbelievers. They feel that if an unbeliever can be doing well, where is their inheritance as believers. They then go to the extent of castigating and denigrating God. I want to tell you that you have nothing to envy in an unbeliever. Have you ever considered that the blades of a fan do not stop turning immediately after the "off" button or switch is pressed? Neither does an iron get cold immediately after it is unplugged from the source of power. You may have a friend, colleague, or Christian brother that seems to be excelling despite committing atrocities; do not copy or envy such, for the fan may have been unplugged from the source of power.

HOW DO WE COAT OUR WEAPON IN CARNALITY?

A great coat for the weapon of many believers is peace. A way to achieve peace is to have your mind focused on the Jehovah Shalom

Thou wilt keep him in perfect peace, whose mind is stayed on thee: because he trusteth in thee (Isaiah 26: 3, KJV)

But many Christians have their minds on the next carrier of news, information, or propaganda. The carrier of gossip prepares cereal, but instead of adding milk, they add bile. After they have deposited the poison, they go to their homes, prepare a nice meal and eat, but you will eat poison and be unable to sleep. You now turn to a pill popper. After swallowing the pill, you still will not sleep, then you start to pray and you expect the prayer to work. The prayer is now of no effect. The tools of your trade have been corrupted.

You may then try to follow God's principle by worshipping him before prayer:

> Enter into his gates with thanksgiving, and into his courts with praise: be thankful unto him, and bless his name. (Psalm 100: 4, NKJV)

The same Word of God that says enter his courts with praise also says "all that is within me."

> Bless the LORD, O my soul: and all that is within me, bless his holy name. (Psalm 103:1, NKJV)

At this time, all that is within you is hatred, turmoil, anger, worry and such. A mind filled with anger, jealousy, hatred, bitterness, and strife cannot bless his holy name. Instead of you sleeping, you become more dejected. A good example is the account of David when he came to Ziklag and found it burnt with fire. All his men started complaining and threatening him. Looking at the situation all around him, he started crying. The more he cried, the more his lieutenants organized to stone him. He then did what caused a turnaround, he forgot about his accusers and insults. He encouraged himself in the Lord; from then on, the situation improved.

To encourage himself in the Lord, he had to take his mind off what the eyes could see, his mind had to be on the Jehovah Saboath. At the time of turmoil or confusion, God just expects you to worship him in spirit and in truth, not be double-minded.

But the hour cometh, and now is, when the true worshippers shall worship the Father in spirit and in truth: for the Father seeketh such to worship him. God is a Spirit: and they that worship him must worship him in spirit and in truth. (John 4:23–24, KJV)

If you are doing it right (i.e. in spirit and in truth), what God just does converts your worship to warfare (mighty through God).

The wilderness and the solitary place shall be glad for them; and the desert shall rejoice, and blossom as the rose. It shall blossom abundantly, and rejoice even with joy and singing: the glory of Lebanon shall be given unto it, the excellency of Carmel and Sharon, they shall see the glory of the LORD, and the excellency of our God. Strengthen ye the weak hands, and confirm the feeble knees. Say to them that are of a fearful heart, Be strong, fear not: behold, your God will come with vengeance, even God with a recompense; he will come and save you. (Isaiah 35:1–4, KJV)

But now I will not be unto the residue of this people as in the former days, saith the LORD of hosts. For the seed shall be prosperous; the vine shall give her fruit, and the ground shall give her increase, and the heavens shall give their dew; and I will cause the remnant of this people to possess all these things. And it shall come to pass, that as ye were a curse among the heathen, O house of Judah, and house of Israel; so will I save you, and ye shall be a blessing: fear not, but let your hands be strong. For thus saith the **LORD** of hosts; As I thought to punish you, when your fathers provoked me to wrath, saith the **LORD** of hosts, and I repented not: So again have I thought in these days to do well unto Jerusalem and to the house of Judah: fear ye not. (Zechariah 8:11–15, KJV)

Your weapon is only made powerful by going to God and not in ganging up.

> There is no king saved by the multitude of an host: a mighty man is not delivered by much strength. (Psalm 33:16, KJV)

> The horse is prepared against the day of battle: but safety is of the **LORD**. (Proverbs 21:31, KJV)

A man once said, "A life can only be understood backwards but must be lived forward." Instead of reviewing our past faults and moving on, we fast-forward every mistake and insult that has happened years ago. No wonder our life is backward. Forget about those things that are behind; it is time to press forward. After the flood, the Rock will still remain.

NUGGETS

- An Insult can propel people to greatness.
- Insult, if properly channeled, can be a fertilizer towards greatness.
- As a Christian, you don't have to start fighting over rights in this world. Our right is to come before God, commit our lives to Him, be obedient to all his instructions, and He will fight your battles.
- Reflect and not Reflex—don't return evil with evil; rather, return evil with good/blessing.
- Insults or ill-will are nothing but weeds among wheat.
- When your approach to insult is negative, you are working against your harvest to either retard or reduce it.
- You must always be hopeful, and not hopeless. Hope does not bring about shame.
- Exercise wisdom and not worry. Wisdom gives peace because you know what others do not know.
- Always be alert and not aloof. Many people have been derailed on their path to greatness because they were too comfortable. Sometimes insults come our way because God wants to keep us on the alert and move us out of our comfort zones.
- Advance in adversity. A time of adversity is a period to adhere to God so that He can advance us. It is a test of our ability to endure.
- When faced with insults or ill will, remember the following:
- For any effective warfare, there has to be weapons (i.e. an instrument of attack or defense in combat).
- Carnality cannot sustain or give longevity to anything.
- Your weapon is only made powerful by going to God and not in ganging up.

PRAYER POINTS

- Lord, help me to turn envy, maltreatment, spite, resentment, hostility and pain to gain, insults to increase, in Jesus' name.
- I choose to advance in adversity. Let every opposition against me activate my destiny in the name of Jesus.
- Daddy, let my focus not shift from you. Help me to always pause to reflect and take the right steps.
- I declare that I will not be put to shame. My hope will not be blown away, and my expectation will not be cut off. After the rainfall let there be sunshine, after my darkness let there be light and after my night let my morning come, in Jesus' name.
- Wisdom that gives ornament of grace and a crown of glory, Father give unto me, in Jesus' name. Amen.
- Lord God of heaven, bless me indeed, enlarge my coast, let your hand be with me, that nothing may grieve me in Jesus' name. Amen.
- God of all comfort, as the sufferings of Christ and the gospel abound in me, let your comfort and love overflow in my life.
- With the mighty weapons of warfare, I pull down every carnality, every stronghold of the enemy in my life and situations in Jesus' name.
- Oh God, clothe me with a garment of praise and worship to continually rejoice with joy and singing in Jesus' name.
- Jehovah El-Shaddai, fight my battles, and give me victory that you have promised, in Jesus' mighty name.

INTEGRITY

Leadership is a combination of strategy and character. If you must be without one be without strategy.

-General Norman Schwarzkopf

And Abimelech said to Isaac, Go away from us, for you are much mightier than we are. So Isaac went away from there and pitched his tent in the Valley of Gerar, and dwelt there. (Genesis 26:16–17, **TAB**)

Integrity is the backbone of greatness. If by freak of nature an individual becomes great (remember greatness is relative) in his own eyes or in the estimation of others, lack of integrity will ultimately cause the demise. Integrity means to be upright or in good moral standing. It involves the conduct of an individual that the Word of God calls holiness. It implies steadfast adherence to a code of conduct or the state of being unimpaired either by what the eyes are seeing or the ears hearing. It simply means being truthful to held beliefs.

Abimelech told Isaac to "go away from us." The reason why he wanted him to go was also mentioned in the passage—"for you are mightier than us." The shocking thing is that Isaac did not contest the declaration and decree of Abimelech. He left the mountain of Gerar for the valley of Gerar. Why was the response of Isaac shocking? Simply, it is the mightier one that should command, not the weaker one. Abimelech recognized Isaac as being mightier. He could easily have organized a coup in Gerar and become the king.

A king called Benhadad was dethroned by one of his officers, Hazael, because of the power of the officer (2 Kings 8:7–15). Benhadad was the king of Syria and at a time he became sick. He sent his servant to Prophet Elisha to find out if he will recover from the sickness. Elisha then told the servant Hazael that the king will die, but Hazael will torment the Israelites. When he got back to his boss, the king, he told the king that he would surely recover from the illness. The next day Hazael murdered the king, and reigned in his stead.

When you compare the story with that of Isaac, you will find out that Hazael was not as mighty as Isaac, and he was a servant, but he still murdered his boss. Isaac, when told to leave, left without any fight, knowing fully well that God is not only God in the mountain of Gerar, but also in the valley and plain. He is omnipotent, omnipresent and omniscient. The integrity of the upright will guide them, while the perverseness of fools will destroy them.

General Charles Krulak, a former commandant of the Marine corps, gave a speech to the Joint Services Conference on Professional Ethics on January 27, 2000:

We study and we discuss ethical principles because it serves to strengthen and validate our own inner value system... It gives direction to what I call our moral compass. It is the understanding of ethics that becomes the foundation upon which we can deliberately commit to inviolate principles. It becomes the basis of what we are... Of what we include in our character. Based on it, we commit to doing what is right. We expect such commitment from our leaders. But most importantly, we must demand it of ourselves.

Sound morals and ethical behavior cannot be established or created in a day... A semester... Or a year. They must be institutionalized within our character over time... They must become a way of life. They go beyond our individual services and beyond our ranks or positions; they cut to the ear and to the soul of who we are and what we are and what we must be... Men and women of character. They arm us for the challenges to come and they impart to us a sense of wholeness. They unite us in the calling we now know as the profession of arms.

Of all the moral and ethical guideposts that we have been brought up to recognize, the one that, for me, stands above the rest... The one that I have kept in the forefront of my mind... Is integrity. It is my ethical and personal touchstone.

Integrity as we know it today stands for soundness of moral principle and character - uprightness - honesty. Yet there is more. Integrity is also an ideal... A goal to strive for... And for a man or woman to "walk in their integrity" is to require constant discipline and usage. The word integrity itself is a martial word that comes to us from an ancient Roman army tradition.

During the time of the 12 Caesars, the Roman army would conduct morning inspections. As the inspecting centurion would come in front of each legionnaire, the soldier would strike with his right fist the armor breastplate that covered his heart. The armor had to be strongest there in order to protect the heart from the sword thrusts and from arrow strikes. As the soldier struck his armor, he would shout "integritas," (in-teg-ri-tas) which in Latin means material wholeness, completeness, and entirety. The inspecting centurion would listen closely for this affirmation and also for the ring that well kept armor would give off. Satisfied that the armor was sound and that the soldier beneath it was protected, he would then move on to the next man.

At about the same time, the praetorians or imperial body-guard were ascending into power and influence. Drawn from the best "politically correct" soldiers of the legions, they received the finest equipment and armor. They no longer had to shout "integritas" (in-teg-ri-tas) to signify that their armor was sound. Instead, as they struck their breastplate, they would shout "hail Caesar," to signify that their heart belonged to the imperial personage- not to their unit - not to an institution - not to a code of ideals. They armored themselves to serve the cause of a single man.

A century passed and the rift between the legion and the imperial bodyguard and its excesses grew larger. To signify the difference between the two organizations, the legionnaire, upon striking his armor would no longer shout "integritas", (in-teg-ri-tas) but instead would shout "integer" (in-te-ger).

Integer (in-te-ger) means undiminished - complete - perfect. It not only indicated that the armor was sound, it also indicated that the soldier wearing the armor was sound of character. He was complete in his integrity... His heart was in the right place... His standards and morals were high. He was not associated with the immoral conduct that was rapidly becoming the signature of the praetorian guards.

The armor of integrity continued to serve the legion well. For over four centuries they held the line against the marauding Goths and vandals but by 383 AD, the social decline that infected the Republic and the Praetorian guard had its effects upon the legion.

As a 4th century Roman general wrote, "when, because of negligence and laziness, parade ground drills were abandoned, the customary armor began to feel heavy since the soldiers rarely, if ever, wore it. Therefore, they first asked the emperor to set aside the breastplates and mail and then the helmets. So our soldiers fought the Goths without any protection for the heart and head and were often beaten by archers. Although there were many disasters, which lead to the loss of great cities, no one tried to restore the armor to the infantry. They took their armor off, and when the armor came off - so too came their integrity" it was only a matter of a few years until the legion rotted from within and was unable to hold the frontiers... the barbarians were at the gates.

Integrity... It is a combination of the words, "integritas" (in-teg-ri-tas) and "integer" (in-te-ger). It refers to the **putting on** of armor or building completeness... wholeness... wholeness in character. How appropriate that the word integrity is a derivative of two words describing the character of a member of the profession of arms.

The military has a tradition of producing great leaders that possess the highest ethical standards and integrity. It produces men and women of character... Character that allows them to deal ethically with the challenges of today and to make conscious decisions about how they will approach tomorrow. However, as I mentioned earlier, this is not done instantly. It requires that integrity becomes a way of life... It must be woven into the very fabric of our soul. Just as was true in the days of imperial Rome, you either walk in your integrity daily, or you take off the armor of the "integer" (in-te-ger) and leave your heart and soul exposed... Open to attack.

My challenge to you is simple but often very difficult... Wear your armor of integrity... Take full measure of its weight... Find comfort in its protection... Do not become lax. And always, always, remember that no one can take your integrity from you... You and only you can give it away!

When Isaac left Gerar, he was wearing the armor of integrity learned from his father Abraham. When Abraham went to rescue his cousin Lot from captivity, he succeeded in not only bringing back Lot, but also the goods stolen. The king of Sodom said to Abram, "Give me the persons and take the goods to yourself." Below is the response of Abram:

> Abram replied, "I have solemnly promised the LORD, God Most High, Creator of heaven and earth, that I will not take so much as a single thread or sandal thong from you. Otherwise you might say, 'I am the one who made Abram rich!' All I'll accept is what these young men of mine have already eaten. But give a share of the goods to my allies—Aner, Eshcol, and Mamre. (Genesis 14:22–24, NLT)

General Krulac said, "my challenge to you is simple but often very difficult":

Wear your armor of integrity
Take full measure of its weight
Find comfort in its protection
Do not become lax

WEAR YOUR ARMOR OF INTEGRITY

As a Christian and good soldier of Christ you should be a vessel unto honor. Your conduct should bring pleasure to the commander in chief (Jesus Christ). Be rugged and cooperate with the master to achieve His purpose. As soldiers in the world have uniforms, so also do Christians. Often times, Christians refuse to wear their uniform. When Samuel started ministering in the house of God under Eli, he was wearing a linen Ephod. God gave the instruction to the children of Aaron to wear fine linen as priests. Now this fine linen is not in the clothing or material, but our conduct because fine linen is the righteousness of saints (Revelations 19:8). Aaron was asked to put on the linen so that his nakedness would not be exposed.

No matter where we find ourselves, if we are wearing our armor of integrity, we will be able to serve, and our nakedness will not be exposed. Do not compromise your armor of integrity in your quest to be great. Keep it polished and shining.

The Bible describes Lucifer as an anointed cherub that had precious gems as his covering. He was cast out of heaven when he exchanged his armor of integrity with that of iniquity. Instead of being positively great he became negatively great.

You were the anointed cherub that covers with overshadowing [wings], and I set you so. You were upon the holy mountain of God; you walked up and down in the midst of the stones of fire [like the paved work of gleaming sapphire stone upon which the God of Israel walked on Mount Sinai]. You were blameless in your ways from the day you were created until iniquity and guilt were found in you.

Through the abundance of your commerce you were filled with lawlessness and violence, and you sinned; therefore I cast you out as a profane thing from the mountain of God and the guardian cherub drove you out from the midst of the stones of fire. Your heart was proud and lifted up because of your beauty; you corrupted your wisdom for the sake of your splendor. I cast you to the ground; I lay you before kings, that they might gaze at you.
(Ezekiel 28: 14–17, **TAB**)

There is a profound statement in the above passage, "I set you so." There is nothing we have in life that has not been given to us by God, and there is nothing we possess that is not His already. "*All things were made by him and without Him was not anything made that was made*" (John 1:3, KJV). Do not get carried away by little achievements and begin to think there is nobody like you. If God should find guilt and iniquity in you, then your journey to greatness may be truncated. Wear the armor of integrity.

TAKE FULL MEASURE OF ITS WEIGHT

Integrity means saying yes to what is right and no to what is wrong. When you decide to take a stand according to the Word of God, there are bound to be opposing views. Take full measure of its weight, do not crumble under the weight. Any stand you take for God is bound to cost you. Let us read a story in Deuteronomy chapter twenty.

When you go forth to battle against your enemies and see horses and chariots and an army greater than your own, do not be afraid of them, for the Lord your God, Who brought you out of the land of Egypt, is with you. And when you come near to the battle, the priest shall approach and speak to the men, And shall say to them, Hear, O Israel, you draw near this day to battle against your enemies. Let not your [minds and] hearts faint; fear not, and do not tremble or be terrified [and in dread] because of them. For the Lord your God is He Who goes with you to fight for you against your enemies to save you. And the officers shall speak to the people, saying, What man is there who has built a new house and has not dedicated it? Let him return to his house, lest he die in the battle and another man dedicate it. And what man has planted a vineyard and has not used the fruit of it? Let him also return to his house, lest he die in the battle and another man use the fruit of it. And what man has betrothed a wife and has not taken her? Let him return to his house, lest he die in the battle and another man take her. And the officers shall speak further to the people, and say, What man is fearful and fainthearted? Let him return to his house, lest [because of him] his brethren's [minds and] hearts faint as does his own. And when the officers finish speaking to the people, they shall appoint commanders at the head of the people. (Deuteronomy 20:1–9, KJV)

There are a couple of lessons to learn from this story. It started off with words of encouragement by Jehovah Elohim through the mouth of Pastor Moses. The passage says: "When," which means of a truth sooner or later we will face difficulties (battles). Irrespective of who we are, there will be one challenge or another that we will have to face. The degree of the battle varies from individual to individual, home to home, corporation to corporation and nation to nation. In most cases the difficulties that we will face will be greater than us physically, but greater is He that is in us than the challenges that we are facing.

Next, we have further encouragement from the priests telling them that they are not alone in the battle, that Jehovah is with them to defeat their enemies. The prerequisite to winning any battle is mentioned by the priest—fear not. When fear comes in, faith goes out. Another important aspect to this story is that encouragement was first given by Moses, the priests, then the officers. The hierarchy of those giving the words of encouragement was diminishing—Moses being higher than the priests and the priests higher than the officers. The officers will be much closer to the people, since the people can easily identify with the officers. In life, sometimes we are able to relate with a word of encouragement if spoken by someone that we know or somebody that has gone through the same thing we are going through.

A friend of mine has a daughter with kidney ailment, and for her to function properly, she was advised to have a kidney transplant. Out of all the members of the family, the right match was my friend. He was eager to have the transplant done, but as with all human beings in a challenging situation like this, you still wonder, "What if..." One day he was taking a stroll, and God used a woman to minister assurance to him. This woman had donated one of her kidneys to her brother, and she was saying that she felt great, the brother even gave her a car as a thank you gift. By the words of this woman, my friend became encouraged. No matter what any pastor had to say, the words of this woman were more comforting because she has been through it before.

> Flatter me and I may not believe you. Criticize me and I may not like you. Ignore me and I may not forgive you. Encourage me and I will not forget you.
>
> -William Arthur Ward

Not only do we have to get encouragement from those close to us but we also need to hear the truth. The officers were saying the stark truth in the Bible passage above:

- Spiritual warfare is not for the feeble minded
- Spiritual warfare is not for those that value humanity above divinity
- Spiritual warfare is not for those that value gold above God
- Spiritual warfare is not for those that value silver above Savior
- Spiritual warfare is not for those that value the terrestrial above the celestial
- Spiritual warfare is not for those that value the ephemeral above the eternal
- Spiritual warfare could lead to death
- Spiritual warfare has benefits
- Its for WARRIORS.

When all the conditions were mentioned, lots of those that enlisted will voluntarily retire from the army. Here comes the wonderful part of the passage (verse 21). When the officers' finish speaking, then will commanders be selected. You have been created to be a commander but you must not be faint-hearted. After the quitters have left, then will the winners be decorated from those that refused to quit. You do not enter a river in winter and say it is cold. Take full measure of the weight. Integrity may cost you, but in the end you will conquer.

FIND COMFORT IN ITS PROTECTION

Integrity is a shield. When you take a stand for God, there will be lots of hues and boos. *"His truth shall be thy shield and buckler"* (Psalm 91:4, KJV).

People will come with different philosophical thinking. The Word of God will even be twisted to make the stand you have taken seem radical. A pastor shared his experience with me a couple of years ago. He took a stand concerning marriage in his church. The Word of God says "marriage is honorable in the bed undefiled." The couple he refused to wed started spreading all sorts of stories about him. At a point, he went to his barber for a hair cut and the barber mentioned that other pastors that were his colleagues and friends that should be defending his stand were speaking ill of him. He was devastated.

A couple of years later, I was also faced with a situation where I had to take a stand for God in the face of everybody. There were lots of talks going around. A wonderful consolation was that immediately after I took the stand on my way home in my car, the Holy Spirit comforted me. *His truth is a shield and buckler.* When Shadrach, Mesach and Abednego stood up while others were bowing down for the image of Nebuchadnezar, they found comfort in the protection of God. He that dwells in the secret place of the Most High shall abide under the shadow of the Almighty. A man of integrity cannot be a pleaser of men.

> My basic principle is that, you do not make decisions because they are easy. You do not make decisions because they are cheap. You do not make decisions because they are popular. You make decisions because they are right.
>
> - Theodore Hesburgh

God has given you a covenant of peace as protection in the face of mockery. He said, "*the mountains shall depart and the hills be removed; but my kindness shall not depart from thee neither shall the covenant of my peace be removed*" (Isaiah 54:10, KJV). He is the supplier of peace. Men may abandon you, but God will embrace you; the peace that God supplies is never ending. Peace in the Hebrew language means shalom, which literally translated means prosperity and wholeness. To guarantee the peace, he sent His only Son also known as the Prince of Peace.

The Prince of Peace said:

These things I have spoken unto you that in me ye might have peace, in the world you shall have tribulation but be of good cheer for I have overcome the world.

(John 16:33, KJV)

Do not give away your integrity.

DO NOT BECOME LAX

Guard your ♡!

To be lax means to let down your guard. We have been enjoined to be sober and vigilant, for our adversary goes about like a roaring lion seeking whom he may devour. He pretends to be a lion, but he is no lion. It is only those that let down their guards that Satan will devour. Do not be lax concerning integrity.

I once heard the testimony of a pastor when he had a bitter disagreement with his wife, and he stormed out of the house. He got into the car and started driving around. This is the kind of opportunity that Satan is looking for. Satan quickly arranged a lady to drive next to him. At the traffic light when it was red, the lady looked at him seductively, winked, and nodded her head in a direction. This was a gesture for him to follow her. The pastor said he was almost driving after her, and he changed his mind all of a sudden. If the pastor had succumbed, it could have meant the end of his marriage, ministry and close relationship with the Lord.

I got an email from a pastor, and below is a warning that he gave based on a real life experience after a ministration:

Giving a ride can be risky— A ride with Jezebel

> Bit I have against thee thou that permittest the woman Jezebel, she who calls herself prophetess, she teaches and leads astray my servants to commit fornication and eat of idol sacrifices... he that has an ear, let him hear what the spirit says to the assemblies. (Revelation 2:20–29, KJV)

"It was a great moment in the presence of God. Signs and wonders were manifested, many captives were set free and a lot of the people in the pew manifested when God's power hit them. Many rolled on the ground and vomited various slimy substances. Pastor Godwin Signs (not real name) was grateful to God. He had thought that the absence of his ministry teammates in the meeting would impede the move of God, but he was pleasantly surprised. As a preacher with a passion for souls, he was excited that more than a dozen people gave their lives to Jesus Christ when he made the altar call. As he stepped down from the altar, he went straight for his car. He pleaded with the host pastor to be allowed to leave as the service ended. He was tired. Exhaustion was etched on his handsome face. So he could not afford to wait longer. Just when the congregation was dispersing, he switched on the ignition of his car and drove through the gate of the massive compound of the church where he had ministered for about ninety minutes that evening.

Two young ladies flagged him down as his car entered the street. He noticed that they were in the church service and therefore stopped. They requested to hike a ride with him. He had no objection. He unlocked the door. Both ladies quickly made an excuse to pick something from the church auditorium. When they returned, one of them had changed her mind. She was going to wait to see her resident pastor. 'I'm only going to drop you at the main juncture since we are not heading for the same direction.' Reluctantly, Pastor Godwin Signs allowed the other lady into his car. 'Thank you sir,' the lady said. The young lady squeezed her small body in the passenger's seat as the car moved on. Yadaw, the latest music of Kunle Ajayi, was blaring in the car while both occupants kept silent.

'I have a problem, sir.' The sister broke the harmony of the instrumental music of Kunle Ajayi.

'What is it about?' Pastor Godwin asked.

'Many men of God have abused me sexually sir,' The lady announced painfully.

'What? What kind of men of God will abuse a young lady like you? I don't think they are men of God,' the man of God retorted.

'They are, sir. I was actually deflowered when one of them raped me some years ago. I met him when he ministered at a program I attended. He was the guest minister.'

'This is not possible. A guest minister raped you after a program. Oh no, the Christian Association and Pentecostal fellowship must hear about this. A man like this must be brought to book for defiling you.' Pastor Godwin could not contain his anger. 'Please give me the man's details.'

'Sir, do I have a seductive spirit? I'm asking because all the men of God who counsel me always make advances at me. Most of them often insist on kissing me the first time I have a close contact with them,' Sister Jessy ignored the request of the man of God.

'If this is the case then you, too, must be careful not to be too close to them. You must protect yourself from being abused sexually.'

In response, the young lady asked, 'Sir, what do you think I should do now? At least three of them have made love to me, and there is one who is currently pestering my life. He has been begging me for a relationship with me for about a year now,' Jessy sounded confused.

'The Bible admonishes us to flee from every appearance of the devil. You must determine in your heart that you do not want to fornicate again. Your body is the temple of the living God. Do not defile it. It is very important that you do not behave in a way that will also make you a prey for the opposite sex. For example, you must stop seeing this so-called man of God who has been chasing you for a year.' Pastor Godwin counseled.

'Do you want to know the truth, sir?'

'Yes, Tell me.'

'I love the pastor. It's just that I respect his wife, sir.'

'You love the pastor!' It was as if a bomb hit Pastor Godwin. 'Are you okay? I think the spirit of Jezebel is upon you. Repent, or you will perish.'

The young lady bowed her head as if in tears. The car pulled to a stop.

'Could you get down now? This is how far I can take you,' Pastor Godwin was disappointed.

The lady was not moved. She rested her head on the head-rest of the seat with closed eyes.

'Madam, kindly alight from this car. My wife is waiting for me at home.' His voiced was raised.

'Your wife? Does she know that you are with me?' Jessy queried.

'Yes, she knows everywhere I am.' His telephone rang. 'Hello my dear, yes. We ended the service some moments ago. I am counseling a sister in my car at the bus stop. I will soon be home... Love you, honey.'

'Do you really love your wife, sir?' Jessy quipped.

'Yes, we love each other.' Pastor Godwin responded.

'I will go down now... Can I make a request sir?'

'Go on please.'

'Will you kiss me before I come down from your car?'

'No! That is a sin. Besides, I don't want to be added to the list of men who have committed adultery with you. Please get down. You are a Jezebel,' Pastor Godwin fumed.

'Is that why you came to disgrace me in church tonight? You made me to roll on the floor several times.' The countenance of Sister Jessy and her voice became violent.

'I rebuke you, Satan! Jesus has spoilt principalities and powers. He has made an open show of you, and you will be forever disgraced in Jesus' name. You foul Jezebel spirit, the Lord rebuke you in the name of Jesus!' He laid his hands on the sister. She was instantly slain in the spirit.

'Please don't use me to preach. Forgive and forget what I have done tonight,' the sister said as the man of God zoomed off in the vehicle."

The just man walks in his integrity. Pastor Godwin had a choice to make, his decision solidifies the assertion of General Krulak, that nobody can take away your integrity. You and you alone can give it away. As much as the daughter of Jezebel tried, the pastor chose the needful one. Choose the needful one. His name is Jesus, and he will keep your steps from falling.

THE NEEDFUL

Now it came to pass, as they went, that he entered into a certain village: and a certain woman named Martha received him into her house. And she had a sister called Mary, which also sat at Jesus' feet, and heard his word. But Martha was cumbered about much serving, and came to him, and said, Lord, dost thou not care that my sister hath left me to serve alone? bid her therefore that she help me. And Jesus answered and said unto her, Martha, Martha, thou art careful and troubled about many things: But one thing is needful: and Mary hath chosen that good part, which shall not be taken away from her. (Luke 10: 38–42, KJV)

Martha and Mary both allowed Jesus into their house, but Mary went to the extent of giving Jesus room in her heart. Jesus entered the house built with hands, but where He really wanted to live is the house built without hands. Martha thought what was needed was service, but what Jesus wanted was submission.

The needful simply means what is required, necessary or indispensable. What is indispensable to Person A may not be indispensable to Person B. It is a matter of opinion and priority. If the question is thrown to different categories of people, a myriad of answers will be received. Answers will range from owning a

Mercedes Benz, eating caviar, sleeping on a waterbed, having an Xbox, paying off debts, going to the moon, receiving healing, etc. The yearning of the heart of every man differs. Some cry for attention while others crave solitude. It ranges from the ephemeral to the eternal (Esau and Jacob). It spans the terrestrial to the celestial.

Due to yearning, leaning or bent of the heart, our perception of situations is sometimes distorted. Where we are supposed to apply wisdom we use emotion. In some other cases, the solution to our situation is right before us and we are not able to recognize it. This is because of wrong expectations or misplaced priorities. Our character and conduct has a direct bearing on our expectations and priorities. Both attributes make up a man of integrity or the lack of it. A man of integrity knows that for everything on earth there is an appointed time, so he is not working to subvert another man or the plan of God. What others call disappointment would really have been appointed from on high.

Is there not an appointed time to man upon earth?
(Job 7: 1, KJV)

For a pig, goat, sheep or cow that is slaughtered, it is a disappointment on the part of the barn mates, but those animals have been appointed for meat.

Thou hast given us like sheep appointed for meat;
(Psalm 44:11, KJV)

Mary chose the needful, which is the word (Jesus), while Martha chose the world (looking good in front of everybody by reason of her service). Jesus is the needful (the main course). The only one that can accelerate your progress on the path of greatness is Jesus. I will advise that you choose him no matter the cloud of witness gathered around you. Make a bold declaration for him, let there be a vital union with him.

You are cleansed and pruned already, because of the word which I have given you [the teachings I have discussed with you]. Dwell in Me, and I will dwell in you. [Live in Me, and I will live in you.] Just as no branch can bear fruit of itself without abiding in (being vitally united to) the vine, neither can you bear fruit unless you abide in Me. I am the Vine; you are the branches. Whoever lives in Me and I in him bears much (abundant) fruit. However, apart from Me [cut off from vital union with Me] you can do nothing.
(John 15: 3–5, TAB)

Because others do not believe the truth of the Gospel of our Lord Jesus Christ or go to church does not wipe out the truth of Gods word. *"For what if some did not believe? Shall their unbelief make the faith of God without effect? God forbid: yea, let God be true, but every man a liar"* (Romans 3: 3–4, KJV).

Do not believe the lie of the devil concerning the promises of God.

You belong to your father, the devil, and you want to carry out your father's desire. He was a murderer from the beginning, not holding to the truth, for there is no truth in him. When he lies, he speaks his native language, for he is a liar and the father of lies. (John 8: 44, NIV)

Counter the lies of Satan with the Word of God. Soak yourself in the Word of God, read books and listen to word tapes and CD's with Godly principles. Surround yourself with people that can positively influence your life. *"So then faith cometh by hearing, and hearing by the Word of God"* (Romans 10:17, KJV).

For I am not ashamed of the gospel of Christ: for it is the power of God unto salvation to every one that believeth; to the Jew first, and also to the Greek. For therein is the righteousness of God revealed from faith to faith: as it is written, The just shall live by faith (Romans 1:16–17, KJV)

Now the just shall live by faith: but if any man draw back, my soul shall have no pleasure in him. But we are not of them who draw back unto perdition; but of them that believe to the saving of the soul. (Hebrews 10: 38, KJV)

Choosing the needful requires absolute obedience.

Saul was looking for popularity, and he neglected the one that could have established him.

And Samuel said to Saul, Thou hast done foolishly: thou hast not kept the commandment of the LORD thy God, which he commanded thee: for now would the LORD have established thy kingdom upon Israel for ever. But now thy kingdom shall not continue: (1 Samuel 13:13, KJV)

Nobody can take the needful away from you except yourself. You can either accept or reject him.

The bread of life was in the house of Martha.

Jesus replied, I am the Bread of Life. He who comes to Me will never be hungry, and he who believes in and cleaves to and trusts in and relies on Me will never thirst any more (at any time). But [as] I told you, although you have seen Me, still you do not believe and trust and have faith. (John 6: 35–36, TAB)

And she was still busy looking for bread.

HOW TO CHOOSE THE NEEDFUL

The needful is none other than Jesus. The Word of God enjoins us to follow His example by considering the Apostle and High Priest of our profession and looking unto Jesus, the author and finisher of our faith. Jesus was in many ways tempted, but yet He was without sin. God himself said, "be holy for I am holy." He furthermore commanded us to follow peace with all men and holiness without which no man shall see Him. While literally "see Him" will mean making it to heaven and enjoying the lovely mansion that has been prepared for us, "see Him" can also mean see His glory. His glory implies favor and greatness. For you to be great you have to be holy. If you have been living holy you cannot afford to stop doing that.

> But anyone who is right with me thrives on loyal trust; if he cuts and runs, I won't be very happy. But we're not quitters who lose out. Oh, no! We'll stay with it and survive, trusting all the way. (Hebrews 10:38–39, MSG)

You have been made right with Him, do not lose that by your conduct. It is a terrible thing to be cast away from the presence of the Lord. Do not cut and run because God will not be happy with you. Imagine a u-turn from love to hatred; to understand what this means we need to look at the life of Amnon and Tamar (2 Samuel 13:1–20). Amnon was the first born of David, and one day a friend (Jonadab) noticed that he was looking dejected, and the friend inquired as to the cause of his demeanor. Amnon poured out his heart that he desired his sister Tamar. The word "desired" here means he wanted to have a sexual affair with her. The friend counseled him on how to achieve his objective. We have to be wary of friends like Jonadab. They are in our lives to test us, and if we fail, they derail us.

Amnon had his way with his sister by raping her. Immediately after the act, the Word of God said he hated her. The love turned to lust. When we cut and run or compromise our stance for God, He will not be happy, and we will eventually be in the history book of losers and quitters. The testimonies of the Lord are very sure. Holiness becomes the house of the Lord.

> I beseech you therefore, brethren, by the mercies of God, that ye present your bodies a living sacrifice, holy, acceptable unto God, which is your reasonable service.
> (Romans 12:1, KJV)

Our body is called the temple of the Lord; therefore we should endeavor not to defile it in any way. Our body is supposed to be a living sacrifice. Do not do with your body what you know God will not be pleased with, and that which goes contrary to His word. Do not defile your body. Daniel said, "I will not defile myself with the portion of the king's meat." The king's meat will be a juicy, hefty and enticing portion, but Daniel eschewed it. What represents the king's meat in your life right now that is beckoning or enticing you? Speak boldly to that thing, "Get thee behind me, Satan." If you fall to the temptation, you may not pay now, but you will pay later. Satan does not give anything free of charge; there is a hefty price to pay. It may not only be earthly greatness, promotion at your place of work, your marriage or a good friend, but it could be the costliest one of all, your own soul. What does it profit a man if he gains the whole world and then loses his own soul?

A major reason why many people compromise the word, or commandments of God, is because they look at others and start to copy them. If somebody is doing something that is wrong, and it seems as if he is "excelling" due to his bad deeds, it does not mean that God has abdicated his throne. Our God is a God that knows. He knows what you do not know, he knows what others do not know, he knows what members of your family do not know, he knows what your friends do not know and he even knows what Satan does not know. He is the only one that knows.

The knowledge of a problem determines how you approach the problem.

The evil person does not experience a good life, so do not compromise. When a man does not fear God, he will fear everything and everybody, including his own shadow. Any slight noise that such a person hears, he believes that people are after him. He is surrounded by bodyguards and leeches always. This is to have a false sense of security. All those around him that he thinks are friends are nothing but parasites. Let things change, and he will see how fast their color will change. The Most High God is an unchanging changer. He is always there in the good and not so good times. So hold onto him.

The promise of greatness to you can only be accomplished if you remain pure.

> With promises like this to pull us on, dear friends, let's make a clean break with everything that defiles or distracts us, both within and without. Let's make our entire lives fit and holy temples for the worship of God.
> (2 Corinthians 7:1, MSG)

Do not light any strange fire like Nadab and Abihu (Leviticus 10:1–10). He will definitely put out the fire. Another name for Him is the consuming fire. If you do not believe, ask Ananias and Saphira (Acts 5:1–11). In our quest for greatness, holiness cannot be trivialized, and our integrity must not be compromised.

NEVER!

> God hasn't invited us into a disorderly, unkempt life but into something holy and beautiful—as beautiful on the inside as the outside. (1 Thessalonians 4:7, MSG)

THE HIGH JUMP PRINCIPLE

In high jump one excellent athlete is needed to jump seven

feet not seven people to jump one feet each.

- Dr. John Maxwell

God is the God of the universe, but he is the father of a few. You belong to him if you do his bidding. His standard may be high, but it is because he wants you to stand out. A friend of mine said, "When others are bowing down, God expects you to stand up. When they are standing up, you are expected to stand out. When they are standing out you are expected to be outstanding. And when they are outstanding you are expected to be the standard." Many are called, but few are chosen. Jesus Christ gave a report to God that out of all he was given he lost none except the son of perdition. God wants us to be children of perfection, not perdition.

It is not about the quantity but the quality.

> God's Message came to me: "Son of man, those who are living in the ruins back in Israel are saying, "Abraham was only one man and he owned the whole country. But there are lots of us. Our ownership is even more certain.' "So tell them, "God the Master says, You eat flesh that contains blood, you worship no-god idols, you murder at will—and you expect to own this land? You rely on the sword, you engage in obscenities, you indulge in sex at random—anyone, anytime. And you still expect to own this land?
> (Ezekiel 33: 23–26, NLT)

Those that are willing and obedient will definitely eat the good of the land. You have a fragrance (an exquisite one). This fragrance goes before you wherever you go, connecting you with favor. It allows you to grow from grace to grace, on your path to greatness. Do not allow it to be the stench of a rotting corpse. Wear your heavenly cologne.

And I got it, thank God! In the Messiah, in Christ, God leads us from place to place in one perpetual victory parade. Through us, he brings knowledge of Christ. Everywhere we go, people breathe in the exquisite fragrance. Because of Christ, we give off a sweet scent rising to God, which is recognized by those on the way of salvation—an aroma redolent with life. (2 Corinthians 2:14–15, MSG)

NUGGETS

- Integrity is the backbone of greatness and requires self-discipline.
- It entails having a good moral standing in the eyes of God.
- The integrity of the upright will guide them, while the perverseness of the fools will destroy them.
- Do not compromise your armor of integrity in your quest to be great.
- Integrity is a shield against unwarranted criticism from men.
- Integrity may cost you, but in the end you will conquer.
- A man of integrity is not a pleaser of men.
- Integrity means living a holy life consecrated unto God.
- Integrity means being the standard and using Christ as the yardstick.
- The knowledge of a problem determines how you approach the problem.

PRAYER POINTS

- Father, make me a person of integrity, in Jesus' name.
- I know you are the same God on the mountain and in the valley. Let your integrity guide and uphold me in Jesus' name.
- Oh Lord, help me to diligently wear my armor of integrity everyday.
- Ancient of days, help me not to soil nor exchange my armor of righteousness.
- Lord, as I take the full measure of the weight of integrity, I will neither be fainthearted nor feebleminded, I will not fear, because I value you more that silver and gold. Help me Lord.
- Heavenly Father, let your covenant of peace and comfort operate in my life, even in the face of mockery.
- Father, I will not be lax with my integrity; uphold me by your grace.
- Father, I refuse to be distracted; I will not be defiled by the king's meat, I will be preserved as a living sacrifice indeed, soul spirit and body.
- Father, I choose to be pure. Help me to be pure so that your promise of greatness upon my life will come to pass, in Jesus' name.
- Lord, I am willing to be obedient, cause me to eat of the good of the land all of my days.

INQUIRE

One of the secrets of life is to keep our intellectual curiosity acute.

- William Lyon Phelps

And Isaac dug again the wells of water which had been dug in the days of Abraham his father, for the Philistines had stopped them after the death of Abraham; and he gave them the names by which his father had called them.
(Genesis 26: 18, NKJV)

Isaac was told to leave his investments in Gerar. Despite his might, he complied. He went to the valley of Gerar, and he started digging, believing all things are possible with God. When you dig, you are making inquiry. Inquiry brings about discovery. In the journey to greatness there could be setbacks, but you should take them as stepping-stones, not stumbling blocks. Your outlook to the situation that you encounter is very important. It may be the difference between wearing the diadem and staying in the dungeon. An inquiry is a close examination of a matter in a search for information, or truth. When you are enjoying divine backing, all things are possible, but you need to make inquiries.

"For with God nothing shall be impossible."
(Luke 1: 37, KJV)

When God is involved in any situation, there is no limit to His accomplishments. Situations that seem impossible become possible. Jesus said He is the resurrection and the life, and He proved it. There was a time when a man's only hope was snatched away by death. This man was called Jairus. To make matters worse, he was very prominent. For eminent people, the hope is that a boy or man will carry on the name of the family, but this man only had a daughter. This girl was very special to him, and death came knocking, but Jesus proved that He is the resurrection and the life. The scientist will always say that for a hypothesis to become a theory and a theory to be a law, it must be proven and repeatable.

Jesus had to prove his name. At another occasion, a woman's only hope was entangled in the jaws of death. As the young man was about to be buried, there was a divine collision. The mourners met with the mighty, the criers met with the champion. All Jesus had to do was touch the coffin. Jesus will not only touch you but also the source of your problem. When the water was bad and the land barren and the report came to Elisha, he touched the water by pouring salt into the water, and the land became healed.

To settle any doubt as to who He is, Jesus demonstrated His name again. This time he allowed a young man called Lazarus to die, to be tied up, buried and stinking so that people would not have any reason to doubt all the miracles he had performed earlier. In the first case, people could say the young girl fainted and that all Jesus did was to revive her. In the case of the widow's son, it could be argued that he was in a coma and the commotion from the crowd awakened him. In the last situation, there was no controversy. Any controversy about you will be settled in Jesus' name. The Word of God that says, "ask" means make inquiries. God has prepared the uttermost part of the earth as an inheritance for you. You need to dig deep.

There is the story of a lady who came to my office about three years ago. She said her husband is a Muslim. They had just been to the doctor, and the doctor had said she could never have a child because her fallopian tube was not right. I asked her if she is a Christian, to which she said, "yes." I told her that with God, nothing shall be impossible. We said a short word of prayer, and that was it. One day I went to a naming ceremony, and as I was leaving a woman came to me and said, "Do you remember me?" to which I said, "No," and then she recounted her story but with a testimony that God had given her the fruit of the womb. The baby will be more than two years old now.

I am positive that irrespective of your situation, inquiry will give you an answer from the Most High. I once heard that in any gathering there are three categories of people, but I will add a fourth category. You identify them by their countenance, their spoken word, and their song.

Those that have just lost a battle:
Outlook: melancholic and morose
Song: It doesn't matter what the eyes do see, it doesn't matter what the ears do hear.

Those that are fighting a battle:
Outlook: aggressive and suspicious
Song: Arise, O Lord, and let your enemies be scattered.

Those that have just won a battle:
Outlook: smiling and rejoicing
Song: Come, let's praise the Lord now.

Those that are living a victorious Christian life:
Outlook: peaceful and glowing
Song: All things are possible.

We can say that Isaac belonged to the last category. His outlook was serene and glowing. His focus was on the strength of God, in spite of the fact that he would have to start from ground zero.

Starting from ground zero requires digging. If you have just been displaced by Hurricane Katrina or Rita, you may be wondering "how am I going to start all over again?" Everything that you have worked for over the years may have been lost. In some cases it could be ancient relics handed over by forefathers or family. The good news is that you are alive, and to him that is joined to the living, there is hope. For with God nothing shall be impossible. The God that made it possible for you to acquire substance is still alive. He does not sleep, neither does He slumber.

There were two families with contrasting situations in the first chapter of the book of Luke:

First family: Zecharias and Elisabeth
Married
Obedient and Blameless
Needed a child
Hopeless
Aged

Second family: Joseph and Mary
Engaged
Young
A virgin woman
Not expecting a child
Just

The statement "For with God nothing shall be impossible" is full of treasures. A lot of times we just mention the statement casually as a cliché. We will take an in-depth look at the statement to enable us understand what Isaac had to go through, and how you can get over any situation that you are facing right now so that you can be all that God intends you to be. Let us dig deep to inquire.

The secret of success is the consistency to pursue
                                           - Harry F. Banks

FOR

The word "for" means completely or in favor, and it has two parts to it—God's part and man's part.

God's Part

When God is for you, it means he is not for you partially, but wholly and whole- heartedly. This is why He said He will neither leave you nor forsake you. The Word of God says, "shall a sucking mother forget her baby," and the response is yes, a sucking mother can forget her baby, but the Lord will never abandon you. This is because you are engraved on the palm of His hands, and your walls are continually before Him. Furthermore He said, "He will carry you even to your old age that He has given birth to you and He will deliver you." These statements from the Lord demonstrate total dedication.

   "For" also means in favor. This is why God said, "His favor will encompass you round about as a shield." His word says Now is the time to favor you. For again means destination (where you are going to), which means He knows where He is leading you. When He is leading you, you can never get lost. He said He will make a way in the wilderness and rivers in the desert.

   The reason why God is for His children is because of His dedication and faithfulness. When God says anything, He is dedicated to its fulfillment. God is interested in the wholesomeness of His children, from the creation of the first man to the death and resurrection of Jesus Christ. We were not only created from dust, He gave us the breath of life so that we can be called a living soul (Genesis 2:7). He went further to empower Adam to name every animal, and whatever name Adam called the animal stuck, it became settled in heaven. Afterwards Adam and Eve messed up, and they were naked and cold, but because of the commitment, dedication and faithfulness of God, He clothed them (Genesis 3:21).

God did not stop there, He was faithful to the word he spoke to Satan that the son of man will bruise your head when the prophet Isaiah said "*For unto us a Child is born and unto us a Son is given*" (Isaiah 9:6, KJV). He did not allow this to remain a prophesy, it came into physical manifestation when the angel Gabriel located a woman called Mary and told her that she is blessed and highly favored and that she has been chosen to bring forth a child whose name shall be called Jesus. Mary questioned the possibility of this when she said, "I am a virgin, I am not yet married, and my husband-to-be is still looking for the bride price. We do not even have a good accommodation. Even if we do get married we are not planning to have a baby right away. What with the cost of taking care of a new born baby." To all these questions, the angel said, "maybe you have not heard about the Holy Spirit, the agent through which impossibilities become possibilities." The rest is history.

When God is for or in favor of a man, He does not stop until His purpose for that individual is accomplished or destination reached. For you and me to be blessed, we have to be His sons and daughters.

> For God so loved the word that He gave His only begotten son so that those who believe in Him will not perish but have everlasting life. (John 3:16, KJV)

Before the above statement could become a reality, Jesus, God's only son, had to die. In His faithfulness, He made sure that this was accomplished. His death alone will not be enough; the way He died was also important to reverse every curse.

> Christ purchased our freedom [redeeming us] from the curse (doom) of the Law [and its condemnation] by [Himself] be-

coming a curse for us, for it is written [in the Scriptures], Cursed is everyone who hangs on a tree (is crucified);

To the end that through [their receiving] Christ Jesus, the blessing [promised] to Abraham might come upon the Gentiles, so that we through faith might [all] receive [the realization of] the promise of the [Holy] Spirit. To speak in terms of human relations, brethren, [if] even a man makes a last will and testament (a merely human covenant), no one sets it aside or makes it void or adds to it when once it has been drawn up and signed (ratified, confirmed). Now the promises (covenants, agreements) were decreed and made to Abraham and his Seed (his Offspring, his Heir). He [God] does not say, And to seeds (descendants, heirs), as if referring to many persons, but, And to your Seed (your Descendant, your Heir), obviously referring to one individual, Who is [none other than] Christ (the Messiah). This is my argument: The Law, which began 430 years after the covenant [concerning the coming Messiah], does not and cannot annul the covenant previously established (ratified) by God, so as to abolish the promise and make it void.
(Galatians 3: 13–17, TAB)

Our freedom was purchased, and every curse was turned into blessing by virtue of the death of Jesus for all those that believe in him. When a human will is made, nobody sets it aside. Compare that to the covenant established by Christ Jesus. It had been drawn up, signed, sealed, delivered and ratified. Look at the summary of Aposte Paul: *"this is my argument the law cannot set aside or annul what has been established by the blood of Jesus."* When you look at how dedicated God is, you will find out that God totally and completely settled His own part of the "for."

He did not mind sacrificing His son as atonement for our sins. He did not mind draining the blood of Jesus so that there will be remission of our sins.

The promise that your children shall be like olive plants round about your table cannot be annulled by the doctor's report. The statement, "Wherever the sole of your feet shall touch, He has given unto you as an inheritance," cannot be annulled by geographical boundaries. The declaration that He will not put any of these diseases upon you cannot be annulled by a feeling or medical report. For by His stripes you have been healed. Hurricane Katrina, Rita, or whatever cannot stop the plan of God for your life. It had already been ratified, signed, sealed and delivered by the precious blood of the lamb.

This was the mindset of Isaac when he left the mountains of Gerar. He knew that before he was born it had already been settled that he would be great because his father Abraham fulfilled his own part of the agreement. The mere words of King Abimelech cannot annul that which God had said. It cannot abolish and make it void. God is for him; this is the reason why the Word of God summarized everything:

> What then shall we say to [all] this? If God is for us, who [can be] against us? [Who can be our foe, if God is on our side?] He who did not withhold or spare [even] His own Son but gave Him up for us all, will He not also with Him freely and graciously give us all [other] things?
> (Romans 8: 31–32, **TAB**)

Man's Part

What almost always holds back the fulfillment of the Word of God in the life of any individual is incomplete commitment to the Word of God. Our commitment must be demonstrated not only by hearing, but also by doing. It must be made manifest by the steps taken and the life of faith lived in unwavering trust. Of a truth, there should be no shadow of doubt that you are for Him. You cannot serve two masters. Isaac took a step of faith. *"But without faith it is impossible to please him for he that cometh to God must believe that he is and that he is a rewarder of them that diligently seek him."* (Hebrews 11:6, KJV) Isaac showed that he is all for God.

> No one can serve two masters. For you will hate one and love the other, or be devoted to one and despise the other. (Matthew 6:24, NLT)

We face situations that cause us to wonder if God is still for us. If we do not look back, God always encourages His children in one form or the other. Jesus Christ, recognizing the propensity of the disciples to doubt Him, had to encourage and challenge them.

> Let not your heart be troubled: ye believe in God, believe also in me. (John 14: 1, KJV)

A house divided against itself cannot stand. If you are for God, let it be apparent to the devil. The devil realized that the man Job was for God. When God divinely displayed Job, Satan retorted that it was because God made a hedge of fire round about him; but Job left no one in doubt that he had decided on whose camp he wants to be a part. Let every member of your household also know that you belong to God. If you know your redeemer is alive, do not act as if He is dead or sleeping or peradventure on a journey. Do not be double-minded. When Isaac left Gerar and he started digging in the valley, I am sure some members of his household were saying behind his back, "We had wells where we were coming from. Why did you leave? You are a weakling," etc. Do not be bothered by the taunting of men. Isaac demonstrated that he was all for God by leaving everything behind and digging a new well.

One thing that is apparent is that when God decides to do something, He goes all out to accomplish His purpose. This shows faithfulness, commitment and dedication. The dedication of God is without controversy. He proved it by ensuring that Jesus Christ died for us so that we might be saved. He intended for us to live a whole and holy life. The question now is how is your commitment? Is it commensurate to that of the Most High God? Are you dedicated to Him at all? Does your action show that you are for Him?

WITH

The word "with" means association, accompanying, alongside, same opinion or belief. A glorious revelation in the action of Isaac when he started digging the well was the realization that he was enjoying divine backing. God was accompanying him. One thing that God loves is company or association. This is one of the reasons why He created you and me. He needed people to relate with and the angels could not fulfill this longing of God because they were not created in the image of God. This is why He boldly declared, "let us create man in our own image." The Bible records that after the creation of the first man and woman, God will come down in the cool of the day to fellowship with them. Furthermore, in the book of Genesis, we see how God enjoyed the company of Enoch.

> Enoch walked [in habitual fellowship] with God.
> (Genesis 5:22, TAB)

> Enoch walked steadily with God. (Genesis 5:22, MSG)

> Enoch lived another 300 years in close fellowship with God.
> (Genesis 5:22, NLT)

From the three translations you see that despite the fact that God was accompanying, alongside or in association with Enoch, Enoch did the same habitually, steadily and closely. Enoch was not forced, coerced or cajoled into serving God. It was free will. He put in his utmost for His Highest. When God knocked on the door of Enoch at times that seemed inconvenient to others, Enoch was ready to be a living sacrifice. Enoch was never late for service (church); before God came to pick him, he was already waiting in the lobby.

Enoch's relationship with God was steady, which means he could be counted on to be at the services. He could be counted on to spend and be spent for the things of God. He had a close fellowship. This translates to the fact that God could trust him and God was also comfortable being around him. He would not spring any surprise. There is the story of a pastor that went to visit one of his parishioners. When the pastor knocked and nobody came to the door, he left his card with the note below:

> Behold, I stand at the door, and knock: if any man hear my voice, and open the door, I will come in to him, and will sup with him, and he with me. (Revelations 3:20, KJV)

In the offering bowl the next Sunday, the pastor found the note below added to his:

> And he said, I heard thy voice in the garden, and I was afraid, because I was naked; and I hid myself. (Genesis 3:10, KJV)

The pastor was able to understand what was going on. You can imagine the look of surprise on the pastor. This was not the case with Enoch. Before God knocked, he already knew another man's wife would not be answering the door. Can you be trusted not to spring a terrible surprise on God?

Jesus Christ recognized the importance of fellowship by following the example of his father in choosing the disciples.

And He appointed twelve to continue to be with Him. (Mark 3: 14, **TAB**)

Your association has a direct impact on your achievement whether positive or negative. Association minus the Almighty equals failure, while association plus the Almighty equals success. In any association, God must be in it. If you are involved in an association or business with anybody, and God did not start it, and He is not continually involved in it, the association will not last. There is nothing wrong in associating, but you must make sure that God sanctions it even though the individual or individuals say they are Christians.

But when the people of Gibeon heard what had happened to Jericho and Ai, they resorted to deception to save themselves. They sent ambassadors to Joshua, loading their donkeys with weathered saddlebags and old patched wineskins. (Joshua 7: 3–4, **NLT**)

Anywhere you step into as a child of God, you are going there with a testimony. "The people of Gibeon heard." Like it or not, people have heard that you are blessed and not cursed. They have heard that there can never be any enchantment or divination against you. I remember when the Spirit of the Lord started whispering to me that I need to go into full time ministry; of course I gave some conditions based on financial consideration. I realized that my income was likely to be drastically reduced initially. So I told God that instead of resigning, I should be laid off due to economic situation. In that case, I would be able to get unemployment insurance until such time as I stabilize as a pastor in full time ministry.

I waited for months on end and also prayed to be laid off but nothing happened until the Spirit of the Lord ministered to me, and He said, "you have passed that stage in your life, nobody can lay you off or fire you." I then knew that I had a decision to make and there can never be any enchantment against me. If the voodooists say they can conjure my spirit up in a mirror or water to do me any harm, the eyes that do that will become blind. As a child of God, you are custom made.

After the fall of the wall of Jericho and defeat of Ai, all the kings of the region combined together to fight against the Israelites, but the people of Gibeon resorted to deception. When people try to derail you and they do not succeed, the next approach is discouragement and deceit by association. Man by nature is always looking for ways to take advantage of another. This is the reason why you have to be "with" God at any point in time or else you may be ridiculed by Satan's ambassadors or emissaries. The ambassadors are well-packaged to fool you no matter your temperament. Joshua momentarily forgot the one that had given him victory and he failed to consult Him before an association was started.

> So the Israelite leaders examined their bread, but they did not consult the **LORD**. Then Joshua went ahead and signed a peace treaty with them, and the leaders of Israel ratified their agreement with a binding oath.
> (Joshua 9:14–15, **NLT**)

Another translation actually says the Israelites partook of their bread.

> So, the [Israelite] men partook of their food and did not consult the Lord. Joshua made peace with them, covenanting with them to let them live, and the assembly's leaders swore to them. (Joshua 9:14–15, **TAB**)

To partake means to involve yourself in, assist or join with. When you join with, you unite (i.e. become one). If you unite with the wrong thing or people, you become defiled. Despite the fact that

₵ HARSH!

Daniel was in Babylon and had the opportunity to really "live it up," he refused to defile himself with the king's meat. A defiled man or woman is already defeated because he has become captive in the net of Satan. Anytime such an individual wants to pray, the accuser is always standing by ready to torment by giving numerous reasons why his prayer cannot be answered.

Do not partake in accepting failure. You have not been created to be a failure. You are not a mistake, neither are you an accident. The fact that you were formed in your mothers womb, made it out of your mothers womb and are still alive today, is a proof of not only your relevance to your generation but also a reference point for generations to come. What you agree with will determine success or stagnancy.

> And Elisha said unto them, This is not the way, neither is this the city: follow me, and I will bring you to the man whom ye seek. But he led them to Samaria.
>
> 2 Kings 6: 19, KJV)

In the passage above we know that the Syrian army was in the city where Elisha also was in order to arrest him. When they asked Elisha if they were in the right city, Elisha said, "No." Can we then say Elisha was lying? The answer is no. He was exhibiting strategic level warfare. He chose not to associate himself with captivity or enslavement. *What you profess, you will possess. What you believe, you are empowered to become.*

The people of Gibeon thought they were master deceivers but they ended up being hewers of wood and drawers of water.

> Bread of deceit is sweet to a man; but afterwards his mouth shall be filled with gravel. (Proverbs 20:17, KJV)

> The light of the righteous rejoiceth: but the lamp of the wicked shall be put out. (Proverbs 13:9, KJV)

"The house of the wicked shall be overthrown: but the tabernacle of the upright shall flourish. (Proverbs 14:11, KJV)

Mark the perfect man, and behold the upright: for the end of that man is peace. (Psalms 37:37, KJV)

The end product of a wrong association is always bitterness. This is why the Word of God says better is the end of a thing than the beginning thereof. Despite the fact that God loves association, he gave a warning: *"associate yourself and you shall be broken, give ear and you shall be broken in pieces."* God is mindful of the effect of wrong association. A king of Judah called Jehoshaphat wrongly had an alliance with the king of Israel called Ahab. They decided to go to war but before going Ahab disguised himself while Jehoshaphat was still clad in his royal garments. The strategy of the opposing army was to kill only the king of Israel. When Ahab and Jehoshaphat went to war, it was only Jehoshaphat that was dressed as a King. The enemy mistook the king of Judah for the king of Israel. During the war, the arrow that was meant for Ahab came looking for Jehoshaphat because he was wearing a royal garment. This is one of the reasons why the Word of God said we must not be unequally yoked—because the tribulation that is not meant for you will start looking for you.

God said, "give ear" because "faith comes by hearing and hearing the Word of God." Faith makes the impossible possible. In the same vein, unbelief comes by hearing and hearing the word of Satan. Unbelief makes possibilities impossible. *What you do is shaped by what you hear and what you hear is determined by who you listen to; who you listen to is determined by who you associate with.* The people you listen to will either build up your faith or destroy it. As children of light, we should always be associated with the Word of God, that is God Himself.

The Word of God is not bound. (2 Timothy 2:9, KJV)

The amplified version says the Word of God is not chained or imprisoned. The message translation says the Word of God is not in jail. This implies that the word is ready to work on your behalf. There is no limit to what the Word of God can accomplish in your life if you associate with the word. He sends his word and His word heals and delivers from destruction. The Word of God is always at attention waiting for our command. The word can never be ambushed so there has to be a deep association with the Word of God. You have a duty to speak the word and stay in the word. Wrong association can uproot the word from you. They can make a mockery of your faith. I have heard many a times that I must be crazy to leave the leeks and the cucumber of secular employment to go into full time ministry but I know whom I have believed.

What if some did not believe and were without faith? Does their lack of faith and their faithlessness nullify and make ineffective and void the faithfulness of God and His fidelity [to His Word]? (Romans 3:3, TAB)

Peoples opinion about you cannot take away the opportunities that God has placed before you. Those that caused the pain of yesterday cannot determine the profit of tomorrow.

The Word of God is God himself and God is a deep God (Romans 11:33). For us to be associated with him, we have to be deep because it is only the deep that can call unto the deep (Psalms 42). If the deep calls on the "not deep," the relationship will not be balanced. At a time, Peter saw Jesus walking on water and he said, "Master bid me come unto you" (KJV). Jesus then asked him to come; when Peter's faith was deep, he could effectively walk on water, but later on he started drowning. When his focus shifted from Jesus, there was an imbalance. The faith of Peter was no longer deep. A good reason why we have lots of challenges as Christians is because we are not deep enough to

Its very uncomfortable to be in an awkward situation / place. - Sept 12th 2022

comprehend the depth of the plan of God and also His commands. God realize that when he gives some commands to us, our actions may drown us. — THAT is challenging!

Do not let your feelings rule your association with God. *Your feeling(s) does not dilute the treasures that God has deposited in you,* neither does present circumstance negate the fact that you are destined for greatness. You should distance yourself from regret. Regret is a sense of loss and longing for someone or something that is gone. *If you keep on regretting your past, you will regress your future.* The psalmist talks about the Israelite exiles sitting down and weeping by the rivers of Babylon. They hanged their harps on the willows, and those that carried them away captive then asked for praise and worship unto the Lord. The exiles could not praise the Lord because they were in a strange land. They had forgotten that God inhabits the praise of his people, and when praise goes up, blessing comes down. *It is during a time of great difficulty that you should praise divinity with great diversity to enjoy great deliverance.*

The psalmist said, "I will praise thee O Lord in good times and in bad times and His praise shall continually be in my mouth." Stop regretting; start responding to the promises of God. *People may know the story of your history but they do not know the glory of your future.* TRUTH!

[handwritten margin note: Is this saying we must go to a foreign land; leaving our native one? — Sept 14 2020]

GOD

The dictionary will describe God as a being conceived as the perfect, omnipotent, omniscient originator and ruler of the universe, the principal object of faith and worship in monotheistic religions. The dictionary cannot really describe who God is. The best description will be found in the Bible, and who He is to you. When you want to know anything about an individual, you start describing the attribute and attitude of the individual.

God is full of compassion. It does not matter who you are, where you are from, where you are going to, and what you are going through, God cares. The care of God for His people is not superficial; it is deeply rooted in love. There are about three different kinds of love (all derived from Greek words):

Eros: This love is based on what the eyes can see or the ears can hear. It is physical or material. It is borne out of carnal desire, based on sexual gratification. It is ephemeral, it only lasts for the duration of the attraction or urge (i.e. what I can get). Immediately after the urge is satisfied, it dies (e.g. 2 Samuel 13:1–17).

Philia: It is based on feelings and it has its root in common experience or ancestry. It exists mostly in siblings (e.g. Genesis 37:4)

Agape: This is a spiritual kind of love. It is not based on what the eyes see. It is an everlasting kind of love. It is sacrificial, unselfish, unmerited and unconditional (e.g. John 3:16).

The agape love is the type that God has for his children. God told the prophet Jeremiah, "I have loved you with an everlasting love."

> Long ago the LORD said to Israel: "I have loved you, my people, with an everlasting love. With unfailing love I have drawn you to myself. I will rebuild you, my virgin Israel. You will again be happy and dance merrily with tambourines. Again you will plant your vineyards on the mountains of Samaria and eat from your own gardens there.
> (Jeremiah 31:3–5, NLT)

Before you were born, God loved you and he still loves you today. His love is unchangeable and unquestionable because He is the same yesterday, today and forever. Sometime ago (in the month of August), I remembered that we had to renew the license plates of our vehicles. When I looked at our financial situation then, I told my wife that God must surely come through for us. After service on a Sunday, a sister came to me and said God told her to give me this envelope for the renewal of our license plate. I said thank you, and I was really excited. I gave the envelope to my wife. Something just came to my mind that I have to see the contents of the envelope. I asked my wife to open the envelope when we got home. Lo and behold there was a check amounting to the cost of the renewal of the license plates of two cars.

It was not the amount of money that really thrilled me but the accuracy of the care and love of God. God knew that we had two cars and this same information was passed to this sister. What a loving God. The love of God means that he can go to any extent to save those that He loves. *When you think your obituary is about to be written, God is preparing your ordination. No matter how many people have forsaken you, or the challenges or difficulties you are going through,* He is the ever-present help, and He had already prepared a way of escape.

> He was amazed to see that no one intervened to help the oppressed. So he himself stepped in to save them with his mighty power and justice. He put on righteousness as his body armor and placed the helmet of salvation on his head. He clothed himself with the robes of vengeance and godly fury. (Isaiah 59:16–17, NLT)

When everybody has abandoned you, God is ready to announce you. God is not afraid to step in. Before you stepped into the trial that you are passing through, the good news is that God stepped in before you. It is because he is there with you that you can still endure. He is the one keeping everything together.

> When the earth goes topsy-turvy and nobody knows which end is up, I nail it all down, I put everything in place again. (Psalm 75:3, MSG)

When the earth totters, and all the inhabitants of it, it is I Who will poise and keep steady its pillars. Selah [pause, and calmly think of that]! (Psalm 75:3, TAB)

The only reason why that child in the hospital is still alive is because God is giving him the breath of life. The husband that is an alcoholic still comes back home everyday because God has need of him. The young girl has not packed out of the house because God knows she may be a Rahab today, but she will bring forth the lineage of the Messiah tomorrow. What are you going through that you are thinking God does not make sense? I want to tell you His ways are not your ways, neither are His thoughts at your level.

I got a call to meet a young man at the subway one day. It was a busy time for me. I tried to convince him to meet me at the church but he said he could not come. I felt the Holy Spirit nudging me to go. Before I left for the appointment, I stopped at the gas station to fill my tank because I was really low on gas. I then went to the subway and met with him. After the meeting, I could only come to the conclusion that I may have wasted my time. At this time, the rain was pouring heavily and I had to wait for a while for it to abate, so that I could dash into my car (I was parked at the pick up area). When I finally got into my car, the traffic was heavy. I turned around to take another route but still met with the same heavy traffic. I kept on inching on gradually. At a time two people came near my car and said I should turn back because there was a particular area that was flooded and cars were submerged; other cars were turning back.

Yours truly kept on going. The rain stopped for a while and I thought before I got to the area where the flooding was bad it would have eased. The journey from the subway to the church office was less than 10 minutes by car, and by this time I had been on the road for about one hour and thirty minutes. When I was about half a kilometer from the area where the road was flooded, it started raining heavily again. I kept on going and a few were turning back. By the time I got to the area where the flood was supposed to be, I encountered dry land. I mean dry land. So that there won't be any doubt as to who is in control, I saw cars that were flooded and the occupants bailing out the water. On the other side of the road, the road was still flooded, but on my side of the road it was dry. Hallelujah!

> Though a thousand fall at your side, though ten thousand are dying around you, these evils will not touch you. But you will see it with your eyes; you will see how the wicked are punished. If you make the **LORD** your refuge, if you make the Most High your shelter, no evil will conquer you; no plague will come near your dwelling. For he orders his angels to protect you wherever you go.
> (Psalm 91: 7–11, **NLT**)

God was only trying to tell me that even floods may arise against me, but He will raise up a standard. He can make a way where there seems to be no way. God will make a way for you in Jesus' name. Amen. Remember that I stopped to fill my tank with gas. God already knew what was ahead; He did not want me to be stranded on the road, in the rain, and in a cold season. He directed me to fill up my tank knowing fully well that it would take me longer than I anticipated.

> Even though others succumb all around, drop like flies right and left, no harm will even graze you. You'll stand untouched, watch it all from a distance, watch the wicked turn into corpses. Yes, because God's your refuge, the High God your very own home, Evil can't get close to you, harm can't get through the door. He ordered his angels to guard you wherever you go. Call me and I'll answer, be at your side in bad times; I'll rescue you, then throw you a party.
> (Psalm 91:7–11, **MSG**)

One wonderful attribute of the Most High God is that he loves to order. This is because He is the Commander-in-Chief of heaven's supreme forces. He is called Jehovah Saboath. What He loves to command is blessing upon His children. He said surely goodness and mercy shall follow you, He also said these blessings shall pursue and overtake you. Goodness and mercy already received a command to follow and they shall continue to follow you in Jesus' name.

You can never get tired of Him because the closer you get to Him, the more you realize that you do not know Him (1 Kings 19: 9–16). He is forever new. Though He is the Ancient of Days, He is not wrinkled and He does not need any make-up or face lift. He is the one that swallowed up death in victory and even asked the grave, "Where is your sting." He did not have hiccups when he swallowed up death. He had no need to take a glass of water because He is the spring of salvation.

Those that do not know Him want to know Him and they cannot stop talking about Him. You may not physically see Him but you can see the work of His Hands. He causes the rain to fall and the sun to shine.

By his knowledge the deep fountains of the earth burst forth, and the clouds poured down rain. (Proverbs 3:20, NLT)

He draws up the water vapor and then distills it into rain. The rain pours down from the clouds, and everyone benefits from it. Can anyone really understand the spreading of the clouds and the thunder that rolls forth from heaven? (Job 36:27–29, NLT)

I kept the rain from falling when you needed it the most, ruining all your crops. I sent rain on one town but withheld it from another. Rain fell on one field, while another field withered away. (Amos 4:7, NLT)

God is not your ward. You are His. You have to do as He says and as He pleases. You always have to make sure your ways and your actions please Him. When a man's ways please the Lord, He makes his enemies to be at peace with him. A way that you can be pleasing unto Him is to do what He desires; that is worship. Worship is not only in singing, but also your lifestyle. Paul and Silas already had a lifestyle that was pleasing to God; that was why they could arise when all others were sleeping in the middle of the night to pray and sing to God. God immediately inhabited their praise. Their jailor became their nurse. He started treating their wounds. Those that have hated you and caused you grief are coming back to beg you in Jesus' name.

Many have tried to taint Him by research but they have become more confused.

> Everything got started in him and finds its purpose in him. (Colossians 1:16, MSG)

> For in much wisdom is much grief and he that increaseth knowledge increaseth sorrow. (Ecclesiastes 1:18, KJV)

Some of us are trying to calculate, permute and "mathematical-ize" God. Listen, because He behaved in a particular way the last time does not mean He will do it the same way the next time. It is only the foolish that will say there is no God. He is the creator of the universe and He does as he pleases. He is self-existing and sovereign. If you take Him to court you are bound to lose. The longest route to a destination with man could be the shortest, safest and best with God.

> When Pharaoh finally let the people go, God did not lead them on the road that runs through Philistine territory, even though that was the shortest way from Egypt to the Prom-ised Land. God said, "If the people are faced with a battle, they might change their minds and return to Egypt." So

God led them along a route through the wilderness toward the Red Sea, and the Israelites left Egypt like a marching army. (Exodus 13:17–18, NLT)

And he brought us out from thence, that he might bring us in... (Deuteronomy 6:23, KJV)

God is not trying to impress anybody, but by the time He steps into a scene, you will have no choice but to keep on echoing His name. He single-handedly fights the battle of His children. The reason why God cares so much about you is because He knows and understands your pain. Have you ever wondered why the Word of God says by His stripes we were healed? Why not by His blood? Why did Jesus get beaten? When you get beaten the way he was beaten, there is a wound, and with time the wound will get healed. Jesus had to go through what it means to be injured, ill or sick. God knows whatever you are going through. To the widow of Zarephath, God knew what she was going through. In her mind she thought she was about to eat her last meal; not knowing that it was going to be the beginning of the best meals for her. In your life it is going to be the beginning of days, weeks and months in Jesus' name.

NOTHING

God loves to make his children happy. This is the reason why He blesses His children. He desires to meet and surpass the expectation of His chosen ones.

Many are the afflictions of the righteous: but the LORD delivereth him out of them all. (Psalms 34:19, KJV)

Whatever situation, problem or difficulty you are facing, God has been in existence before the trial and He knows the life cycle of the trial.

Fear nothing that you are about to suffer. [Dismiss your dread and your fears!] Behold, the devil is indeed about to throw some of you into prison, that you may be tested and proved and critically appraised, and for ten days you will have affliction. (Revelation 2:10, TAB)

Before the mountains (trials) were formed, He has been God. The level of understanding that an individual has about a situation will determine his approach to the situation. The Word of God says that affliction does not spring from the dust (i.e. there is a root cause to every difficulty, and he that breaks the hedge, the serpent shall bite).

There was a time when there was war in heaven. Jesus was the representative of the heavenly host. Jesus Christ used His word to withstand all the tempting offers of Satan. He responded with the undiluted and unadulterated Word of God to all the overtures of Satan. Remember that all Satan goes about doing is to kill, steal and destroy; when you fall prey to him, he will now be able to accuse you. In a court of law, there is the plaintiff and the respondent. Based on the arguments, witnesses and evidence put forward, one of them is declared either innocent or guilty. Satan in this case was the plaintiff; he was busy accusing Jesus to ensure that He fail, and He is pronounced guilty. As much as Satan tried, he could not lure Jesus to sin. Jesus did not succumb to the lust of the eyes or flesh. He upheld His integrity. The last card that Satan had was to incite Jesus to fight him but Jesus kept his peace and waited on the word that says "vengeance is mine I will repay says the Lord."

Therefore, Jesus was able to pronounce Himself innocent because He said, "The prince of this world came, and found nothing in me." Automatically somebody else must be guilty; that is Satan. Not only is somebody else guilty but something was also found in the guilty one before he could be pronounced guilty. This means there was no basis for affliction, sickness, diseases, lack, etc. to attack Jesus. They cannot be found in him. When diseases, etc. tried to attack Jesus, all he had to say was nothing. This implies that Jesus has legal authority to tell affliction in all its ramifications to clear out. It is one thing to have authority, it is another thing to have the mindset of one that has authority. Due to the innocence of Jesus, His view (mindset) of problems, illness, poverty, etc. is different. He regards them as something that is of no consequence or significance.

When you succumb to sin, it adds a whole family of sorrow to you (e.g. fear, worry, unbelief etc.). In the case of Jesus, fear, worry or unbelief had no part with him. Whatever difficulty he encountered, he regarded them as nothing because he had no capacity to doubt the power of his Father. The seed that will cause calamity to grow was not found in Him; the only thing in Him is the incorruptible seed. When you make something or someone important, they start to act and manifest importantly. Whatever the situation encountered by Jesus, it could not change His belief. Jesus refused to transfer, sell or give the title deed of His authority to the situations He encountered. He recognized that He is from above and He is above all.

Against this background we can describe the word "nothing" as follows:

Something that has a quantity of no importance; nonentity

He went back into the palace and said to Jesus, "Where did you come from?" Jesus gave no answer. Pilate said, "You won't talk? Don't you know that I have the authority to pardon you, and the authority to—crucify you?" Jesus said, "You haven't a shred of authority over me except what has been given you from heaven. That's why the one who betrayed me to you has committed a far greater fault. (John 19: 9–11, MSG)

When Jesus came before Pilate, He regarded him as a nonentity, somebody that could not change the course of His life or destiny. He told him directly, "listen you cannot do anything about me." At a time, before Jesus Christ even spoke, He was just looking at Pilate. Sometimes silence is a good answer for a fool. Do not water the seed of affliction. Isaac regarded the task before him as nothing.

Something that has no existence

> One of those days He and His disciples got into a boat, and He said to them, Let us go across to the other side of the lake. So they put out to sea. But as they were sailing, He fell off to sleep. And a whirlwind revolving from below upwards swept down on the lake, and the boat was filling with water, and they were in great danger. And the disciples came and woke Him, saying, Master, Master, we are perishing! And He, being thoroughly awakened, censured and blamed and rebuked the wind and the raging waves; and they ceased, and there came a calm. (Luke 8:22–24, TAB)

Faith teachers have taught us that if you can see it, you can receive it. It is the same logic that fear works with. If you can see fear you can also receive it. Job always saw the calamity that would befall his family, and he later received the tragic news. Jesus already pronounced to his disciples that they were going to the other side. In His mind He already saw the other side. He did not see the storm at all. This is the reason why He could safely sleep. *When the disciples were questioning His love for them, He was questioning their faith in His word.* If Jesus said you are going to the other side, you better believe it; a thousand and one demons cannot stop you except you decide to stop yourself.

Nothing will stop us.

Something that has no quantitative value; zero, nada, nil, zilch

> Jesus soon saw a great crowd of people climbing the hill, looking for him. Turning to Philip, he asked, "Philip, where can we buy bread to feed all these people?" He was testing Philip, for he already knew what he was going to do. (John 6:5–6, NLT)

When the disciples looked around, they saw a great multitude. Many things were going through their minds, but to Jesus, *the quantity of the multitude had no value compared to the quality of the Master.* In the same vein, *the volume of the problem you are facing has no veracity compared to the victory you are going to experience in Jesus.* The bigger they are, the more the sound they will make when they fall.

Something of no consequence, significance, or interest

> When Jesus received the message, He said, This sickness is not to end in death; but [on the contrary] it is to honor God and to promote His glory, that the Son of God may be glorified through (by) it. Now Jesus loved Martha and her sister and Lazarus. [They were His dear friends, and He held them in loving esteem.] Therefore [even] when He heard that Lazarus was sick, He still stayed two days longer in the same place where He was. (John 11:4–6, TAB)

Because there is a delay does not mean you have been denied. He that will come will still come. Jesus proved that His name is the resurrection and the life. No matter the situation that you are facing, there can still be resurrection. Dry bones can live again.

When divinity looks at a problem or difficulty, the conclusion reached is nothing.

> Behold, I am the LORD, the God of all flesh: is there any thing too hard for me? (Jeremiah 32:27, KJV)

But when humanity looks at the same situation, the conclusion reached is something.

> And they brought up an evil report of the land which they had searched unto the children of Israel, saying, The land, through which we have gone to search it, is a land that eateth up the inhabitants thereof; and all the people that we saw in it are men of a great stature. And there we saw the giants, the sons of Anak, which come of the giants: and we were in our own sight as grasshoppers, and so we were in their sight. (Numbers 13:32–33, KJV)

Humanity makes a mountain out of a molehill because we allow something to be added to us in the form of fear and unbelief. Paul the apostle declared:

> But of these who seemed to be somewhat, (whatsoever they were, it maketh no matter to me: God accepteth no man's person:) for they who seemed to be somewhat in conference added nothing to me: (Galatians 2:6, KJV)

Since nothing negative is being added to the King of Glory. He is able to see every difficulty as nothing. A parallel is how God turns failure to success. When two individuals (A and B) with the same ability are given two rooms, Y(full) and Z(empty) respectively, to furnish with the same amount of furniture, and at a given time (a test of efficiency), the probability of individual B filling up room Z faster than individual A is higher because the room is empty, while individual A has to first empty room Y before he can fill it up.

This is exactly the way that God deals with us. We need to first empty ourselves of unbelief, fear, anger, animosity, anxiety, etc. before the glory of the Lord can fill our lives. This is why the Word of God says that there must first be a transformation.

> Don't copy the behavior and customs of this world, but let God transform you into a new person by changing the way you think. Then you will know what God wants you to do, and you will know how good and pleasing and perfect his will really is. (Romans 12:2, **NLT**)

When you begin to copy, you are adding what should not be in you to yourself. What you add to yourself controls you (e.g. alcohol, drugs, sexual immorality, inordinate affection, etc.). You transfer your God-given authority to what you have added to yourself that is now controlling you. The reason why God could not do anything with the ten spies was that they transferred their royalty and peculiarity to the sons of Anak—"and so were we in their sight." Remember, they were spies, which means the inhabitants of the land did not see them or else they would have been captured.

Naomi said, "Do not call me Naomi again." She said, "I went out full but the Lord has brought me home again empty, why then are you calling me Naomi, seeing the Lord has testified against me and the Almighty has afflicted me." Naomi went with two sons and a husband. In her own mind she was full, but in the sight of God, she was full of mediocrity when all God intended for her was to be filled with excellence. Many are the afflictions of the righteous but God delivered him from all of them.

Your perception of a situation will ultimately determine its potency.

And when the servant of the man of God was risen early, and gone forth, behold, an host compassed the city both with horses and chariots. And his servant said unto him,

Alas, my master! how shall we do? And he answered, Fear not: for they that be with us are more than they that be with them. (2 Kings 6:15–16, KJV)

The servant of Elisha said, "How shall we do?" Ordinarily when you are faced with a difficult situation you say, "What shall we do?" The statement "How shall we do?" could either be based on fear or faith. If based on faith, it means "How are we going to destroy the enemies facing us?" Is it by calling fire on them just like Elijah did, by asking the ground to open up and swallow them just like in the case of Dathan, Korah and Abiram, or by asking a she bear to devour them as Elisha did. If it is fear-based; it could mean "What route should we take to escape; do we jump from the roof or go through the sewage pipes."

In the case of the servant, it was obviously fear-based because Elisha said, "do not fear for they that are with us are more than the enemies you are seeing." Elisha saw them as nothing. He did not allow Satan to add fear to him. Elisha knew he was serving a God that is able, whose testimony is sure. The God that has done it before is also able to do it again, because He is the same yesterday, today and forever. Whatever challenge you are facing, try and remember the victory that God has given you before. The God that allowed you to conquer that situation has not been dethroned. When King Uzziah died, Isaiah saw also the Lord sitting on the throne. God is sure of his power; therefore he is not running helter-skelter. He is able to deal with any situation. No matter the name or category of your problem, God is able to deal with it and he has never been defeated so without a doubt you are in the winning camp. You will win in Jesus' name.

The unbelief has to go out for victory to come in

And He brought us out from there, that He might bring us in to give us the land which He swore to give our fathers. (Deuteronomy 6:23, TAB)

PURGE YOURSELF OF THE FOLLOWING:

Animosity

The desire of God is for brotherly love to continue and not hatred.

> And may the Lord make you to increase and excel and overflow in love for one another and for all people, just as we also do for you, So that He may strengthen and confirm and establish your hearts faultlessly pure and unblamable in holiness in the sight of our God and Father, at the coming of our Lord Jesus Christ (the Messiah) with all His saints (the holy and glorified people of God)! Amen, (so be it)!
> (1 Thessalonians 3: 12–13, **TAB**)

Anxiety

When there is a feeling of apprehension, you are double-minded and you cannot receive from the throne of grace.

> Do not fret or have any anxiety about anything, but in every circumstance and in everything, by prayer and petition (definite requests), with thanksgiving, continue to make your wants known to God. And God's peace [shall be yours, that tranquil state of a soul assured of its salvation through Christ, and so fearing nothing from God and being content with its earthly lot of whatever sort that is, that peace] which transcends all understanding shall garrison and mount guard over your hearts and minds in Christ Jesus.
> (Phillipians 4:6–7, **TAB**)

Anger

A man that is full of rage cannot make intelligent decisions.

The decision that you make when angry is based on a desire to payback (vengeance).

> But now put away and rid yourselves [completely] of all these things: anger, rage (Colossians 3:8, **TAB**)

> Don't be quick-tempered, for anger is the friend of fools. (Ecclesiastes 7:9, **NLT**)

SHALL BE IMPOSSIBLE

The word "shall" could mean:

Something that will take place or exist in the future.

> The people I formed for myself, that they may set forth My praise [and they shall do it]. (Isaiah 43:21, **TAB**)

> The people I made especially for myself, a people custom-made to praise me. (Isaiah 43:21, **MSG**)

One thing that is guaranteed about you is that you will praise the King of Glory if you continue to hold unto Him and operate according to His laid down principles. It is guaranteed to happen because you have been created or custom made for such a purpose. I was driving on the highway one day and I saw an antique car shining and speeding along the highway. The license plate of the car said OUR 52. Subconsciously I became careful about my driving because certain things were going on in my mind. It is an uncommon car. The auto-mechanics for such a car are uncommon. The owners of such a vehicle are uncommon. The spare parts for such cars are uncommon. To sum everything up, it has been custom made and it is now glittering wherever it goes. The same applies to you as a Christian. You are uncommon, your

Creator is uncommon, and your spare parts are uncommon. You are custom made.

Looking at the *our* 52 vehicle, many like it would have been thrown into the junkyard but somebody decided to do some special work on that particular one to make it uncommon. When you look at some of your friends or colleagues, you will see that some have passed away or we can say some are in the "junkyard" hooked on drugs. You are what you are today by the special grace of God. You are still alive because God has decided that you shall show forth His praise, He is doing some special work on you. This is the reason why He said:

> You didn't choose me, remember; I chose you, and put you in the world to bear fruit, fruit that won't spoil. As fruit bearers, whatever you ask the Father in relation to me, he gives you. (John 15:16, MSG)

A salient word with meaning in the above verse is "remember." I want you to remember everything you have passed through in life. Were you in the Twin Towers when the terrorists hit the building? Were you in Indonesia when the Tsunami struck? How about the Air France Jet that overshot the runway at Pearson International Airport, Toronto, or the Hurricane that ravaged the Gulf coast and leveled Mississippi, New Orleans and Mobile, Alabama? After all these setbacks, you are still alive and progressing. Many times in the scripture you will read the statement "and it came to pass." All these incidents came into existence to pass away so that they will not keep on threatening your future. You are more than a conqueror. You will live and not die to declare the goodness of the Lord.

Something that is a promise or obligation

> For you shall go out [from the spiritual exile caused by sin and evil into the homeland] with joy and be led forth [by

your Leader, the Lord Himself, and His word] with peace; the mountains and the hills shall break forth before you into singing, and all the trees of the field shall clap their hands. (Isaiah 55:12, **TAB**)

Whatever God has said, He will do. He will surely do. If God has said you are going out of captivity, it is already done. He speaks and it is done. He commands and it stands. The book of *Basic Instructions Before Leaving Earth* is filled with promises for the children of God. With the promises are conditions. There is nobody that has complied with the conditions of God that has not been blessed. A wonderful example is the father of faith, Abraham. He was told to leave his country, kindred and his father's house with the promise of awesome blessings if he obeyed. **You compel the hand of God to move on your behalf when you obey him.**

In the past couple of weeks the price of gas has soared to alarming proportions but do not let that curtail your service to God. The silver and gold still belongs to God and He is also the oil magnate. At this time you need to **guard your heart with all diligence because out of it ensues the issues of life. Check the train of your thoughts.** Silence negativity. God already said, "you shall go out." And you will go out of poverty in Jesus' name. God has decreed; it nobody can annul it. Isaac was sent out of the mountains of Gerar and he went out with joy and was led forth in peace. He started digging (i.e. making inquiries). Though he met obstacles, he knew that God who has promised would definitely fulfill his promise. Keep on digging.

Something that is inevitable

That the dream was sent twice to Pharaoh and in two forms indicates that this thing which God will very soon bring to pass is fully prepared and established by God. (Genesis 39:32, **TAB**)

The word "inevitable" means impossible to avoid or prevent. It is like planting a good seed in a good soil; the seed will surely germinate. It is bound to produce. You have been programmed to excel in life no matter what you are going through and the challenges before you. Joseph was already programmed to excel; it was just a matter of time. No divination or enchantment could stop the plans of God for him. The dungeon could not stop it; neither could the dragons. Going back to the analogy of the good seed in the good soil, do you know that when the seed begins to germinate, rodents and parasites can cut its life short? In your own case as a child of God, since you are his planting and he has purposed to bless you, no Balaam or Balak can curse you.

> "Thus says the Lord of hosts: In those days ten men out of all languages of the nations shall take hold of the robe of him who is a Jew, saying, Let us go with you, for we have heard that God is with you."(Zechariah 8:23, **TAB**)

God says that He has purposed to do you good. When others are talking about a casting down, a lifting up is your portion. One thing that is inevitable is the defeat of your enemies. My brothers and sisters, the defeat of that cancer, HIV, sickle cell anemia, stillbirth, failure at the edge of success, delayed blessings, and purposeless living is inevitable. By His stripes you were healed. Your healing had been given to you more than two thousand years ago. Receive it as you read this book today in Jesus' name. Amen. The woman with the issue of blood said, "If I can only touch the hem of His garment." All you need is a touch from the supernatural.

Something that has the ability to accomplish

> See now that I, even I, am he, and there is no god with me: I kill, and I make alive; I wound, and I heal: neither is there

any that can deliver out of my hand.

(Deuteronomy 32:39, KJV)

A young man once narrated the story of his childhood, how his mother used to literally slave to send them to school. The father died at a young age, they had to hawk sewing utensils to go to school. During his final year in the university, he used to eat once a day. About a week to his final exam, he had a minimal amount of money with him that was not enough for him to eat once a day. As he finished his final exam, he fainted due to lack of food. The mother of this young man was very loving and caring; she wished she could adequately take care of the children, but she did not have the power (financially). She wished she could, but she did not have the means. Not only does God wish, He can also do. He is the one that works both to will and to do according to His good pleasure.

A similar story is of a widow of one of the sons of the prophets (1 Kings 4:1–7). She wanted to take care of her sons and pay off her husband's debts, but she did not have the ability. One day she came across the ability carrier in the person of Elisha and things changed. Your situation will change today in Jesus' name. Amen.

When you look at situations all around, you can start wondering what is going on. This is the time that you need kingdom mentality because the ability of God has not diminished. There was a time that the prophet Jeremiah was pleading his case before God, asking God to do something about his situation. The response of God was shocking. God simply told him to have kingdom mentality.

[But the Lord rebukes Jeremiah's impatience, saying] If you have raced with men on foot and they have tired you out, then how can you compete with horses? And if [you take to flight] in a land of peace where you feel secure, then what will you do [when you tread the tangled maze of jungle

haunted by lions] in the swelling and flooding of the Jordan?
(Jeremiah 12:5, **TAB**)

The Lord rebuked Jeremiah's impatience. I am sure Jeremiah would have been shocked to his bone marrow. He thought God would organize a pity party for him. The El Shaddai God came out bluntly. How much heat you are willing to endure will determine how high you will rise. Everything precious comes from pressures. There is a required quality for greatness in life and it is kingdom mentality. It is time for his children to walk by faith and not by sight. He is still the All Sufficient God. Caleb exhibited this mentality at the age of eighty years when he told Joshua to "give me this mountain." He was not depending on his aptitude but the ability of God. It is time to put Satan where he belongs. There is the story of a New York attorney that went visiting in Texas and he killed a deer. As he got out of his car to pick up the animal, a farmer accosted him. The farmer said the lawyer cannot pick the animal, since the animal was killed on the farmer's land. The attorney started raving and ranting that he would sue the farmer. The farmer then told him about a three-hit rule in Texas. The farmer said one of them will hit the other three times, then the other person will also hit three times. This will go on until one of them withdraws. The person that wins takes the deer.

The farmer chose to hit first. He punched the lawyer once and this lawyer sprawled on the floor. The second time he hit the lawyer, the lawyer was dazed. At this juncture, because the lawyer was younger, heavily built and supposedly stronger, he was thinking one more hit and it would be his turn to flatten the scrawny farmer. On the third occasion, the farmer leveled the lawyer. Painfully, with every bone creaking, the lawyer got up ecstatic that it is now his turn. As he was getting ready to kick the farmer, the farmer said he was withdrawing from the contest and that the lawyer can keep the deer—kingdom mentality. Wisdom is better than weapons of war. It is time for you to kick the devil because he is under your feet. The price of gasoline could be two dollars per liter or four dollars per gallon. As a child of God there will be divine sustenance. Heaven's bank will never run dry. It is impossible.

When God sees that the price is getting too high, because of His children, a decree will be made that will cause the price to drop. God has the ability because the heart of the president, prime ministers and legislators are in His hands. He can turn it wherever He wants. All you need is His favor. I disagree here. If God doesn't have their O7, they will not obey him.

> And may I have a letter to Asaph, keeper of the king's forest, so he will give me timber to make beams for the gates of the citadel by the temple and for the city wall and for the residence I will occupy?" And because the gracious hand of my God was upon me, the king granted my requests.
> (Nehemiah 2:8, NIV)

The knowledge of the power of God enabled Isaac to dig (i.e. make inquiries). Whatever you are facing in life, make inquiries and you will discover that with God nothing shall be impossible.

> Say not thou, What is the cause that the former days were better than these? for thou dost not enquire wisely concerning this. (Ecclesiastes 7:10, KJV)

NUGGETS

- Inquiry brings about discovery.
- Man by nature is always looking for ways to take advantage of one another.
- A defiled man is already defeated because he has become captive in the net of Satan.
- What you profess, you will possess. What you believe, you are empowered to become.
- Faith makes the impossible possible, while unbelief /fear makes possibilities impossible.
- What you do is shaped by what you hear, and what you hear is determined by who you listen to. Who you listen to is determined by who you associate with. Who you listen to will either build up your faith or destroy it.
- If you keep on regretting your past, you will regress your future.
- People may know the story of your history, but they do not know the glory of your future.
- God is not your ward. You are His.
- The level of understanding that an individual has about a situation will determine his approach to the situation.

PRAYER POINTS

- Father, let every setback in my life become stepping stones to my greatness in Jesus' name.
- Oh Lord, settle every controversy about my greatness today, in Jesus' name.
- I refuse to succumb to sin, for sin shall not have dominion over me, in Jesus' name.
- God, you are a winner; in this race of life, make me a winner indeed; in the race to greatness let me be victorious, in the race to heaven, make me an overcomer, in Jesus' name. Amen.
- Ancient of Days, guide me when digging. My inquiries will not be in vain, my time and efforts will not be wasted, in Jesus' name.
- Lord, you have purposed to do me good, let the good come now.
- I purge myself of every animosity, anger and anxiety that may hinder my digging in Jesus' name.
- You are the God of the impossibility; make every impossibility a possibility in my life in Jesus' name.
- All my problems are nothing to You; make them nothing to me indeed in Jesus' name.
- Abba Father, because You are for me, lead me into greatness, in Jesus' name.

IMPACT

Think like a man of action, act like a man of thought.

- Henry Bergson

One day, as Isaac's servants were digging in the valley, they came on a well of spring water. The shepherds of Gerar quarreled with Isaac's shepherds, claiming, "This water is ours." So Isaac named the well Esek (Quarrel) because they quarreled over it. They dug another well and there was a difference over that one also, so he named it Sitnah (Accusation). He went on from there and dug yet another well. But there was no fighting over this one so he named it Rehoboth (Wide-Open Spaces), saying, "Now God has given us plenty of space to spread out in the land. (Genesis 26:19–22, MSG)

Impact can be described as the power of making a strong and lasting impression. Resiliency and perseverance have a big part to play in impression. Success does not happen by accident. It is always by design. Isaac did not allow quarrel or accusation to dissuade him from making an impact. The hypostasis of impact is input. Every action of Isaac was well planned. He was working according to a heavenly script. Another meaning of impact can be likened to the striking of two objects against each other. When Isaac dug the first well that developed into a quarrel, a quarrel arose because the noise made from the impact of the implements used in digging and the force of the water gushing out was not loud enough, but when he dug the last one, the vastness of the well and the force of the spring of water silenced the cantankerous people. Excellence will always silence detractors. This is the reason why the Word of God says whatever your hand finds to do, do it well. One important thing that you find in the life of Isaac is that he never allowed controversies to hold him back. He refused to trade with mediocrity. *When whatever you have is good enough, people will listen to you.* Let us look at the story of a man that was born blind.

> As Jesus was walking along, he saw a man who had been blind from birth. "Teacher," his disciples asked him, "why was this man born blind? Was it a result of his own sins or those of his parents?" "It was not because of his sins or his parents' sins," Jesus answered. "He was born blind so the power of God could be seen in him. All of us must quickly carry out the tasks assigned us by the one who sent me, because there is little time left before the night falls and all work comes to an end. But while I am still here in the world, I am the light of the world." Then He spit on the ground, made mud with the saliva, and smoothed the mud over the blind man's eyes. He told him, "Go and wash in the pool of Siloam" (Siloam means Sent). So the man went and washed, and came back seeing! (John 9:1–7, NLT)

The ministry of Jesus without a doubt was that of impact. By the power of the Holy Spirit, He went about doing good. One day He came across a man that was blind from birth. and He was asked lots of questions as to the reason why the man was blind, but Jesus answered all questions with impact. He spat on the ground, made mud with the saliva and smoothed the mud over the man's eyes. One thing that is sure is that everybody would have been talking about His unorthodox way of healing. The former blind man also had impact answers for those wondering about him. He came out boldly to say I am the one that has been healed. When he was again asked if he knew that the one who healed him was a sinner, his answer was also full of impact. *"Whether he be a sinner or no, I know not: one thing I know, that whereas I was blind, now I see."* (John 9:25, KJV). Your spoken word is a treasure. When you talk, people have a glimpse of your mind (i.e. your intelligence and integrity quotients). You must not talk to be heard but to make impact. Many people have the right to talk but it is not all that have earned the right to be listened to.

There are lots of actions in life that go unnoticed but some actions are not only noticed by the present generation but also by generations yet unborn. Anything that you do must be with impact for you to make a difference in life. With impact you stand out and without it you blend in. Impact is not gaining popularity or seeking attention; neither is it showboating. It simply means doing everything to make a lasting mark.

> I found that the men and women who got to the top were those who did the jobs they had in hand with everything they had; energy, enthusiasm and hard work.
>
> - Harry S. Truman

Jehovah is a God of impact. God appeared to a man called Moses in the mount of Horeb, the bush was burning without being consumed. This drew the attention of Moses. Later, Moses was sent to the king of Egypt. Pharaoh, after much hardship, allowed the Israelites to leave Egypt to serve God. In case you have read the story before and you are wondering, how come Pharaoh did not allow the Israelites to leave with all the dreadful events that happened in Egypt? The answer is God was working according to a script. God never does anything haphazardly. Everything he does is well planned out. He said he had hardened the heart of Pharaoh so that His power will be shown to the world through him. This statement can be explained through the Word of God that says, "He has put a plan in their mind, a plan to achieve His purpose." For you to live a life of impact, you must have a plan, then pursue the plan with passion.

Let us look at an excerpt from the Oxford dictionary of Scientists about Albert Einstein (1879–1955) German–Swiss–American theoretical physicist:

Einstein was born at Ulm in Germany where his father was a manufacturer of electrical equipment. Business failure led his father to move the family first to Munich, where Einstein entered the local gymnasium in 1889, and later to Milan. There were no early indications of Einstein's later achievements for he did not begin to talk until the age of three, nor was he fluent at the age of nine, causing his parents to fear that he might even be backward. It appears that in 1894 he was expelled from his Munich gymnasium on the official grounds that his presence was disruptive. At this point he did something rather remarkable for a fifteen-year old boy. He had developed such a hatred for things that are German that he could no longer bear to be a German citizen. He persuaded his father to apply for a revocation of his son's citizenship, a request the authorities granted in 1896. Until 1901, when he obtained Swiss citizenship, he was in fact stateless.

After completing his secondary education at Aarao in Switzerland, he passed the entrance examination at the second attempt, to the Swiss Federal Institute of Technology, Zurich, in 1896. He did not appear to be a particularly exceptional student.

One thing that can be deduced from the above biography is that Albert Einstein did not show particular brilliance in his early years. He made a decision that had a great impact on his life at the age of fifteen. He revoked his German citizenship. He then went on to complete his secondary education. After making that decision, he started making progress according to a script he had written in his mind. He had a plan with a purpose and he diligently pursued it. His life was full of setbacks because in many instances he would pass at the second attempt or not get what he applied for, but he still pursued. Your decision will determine your distinction. For a life of meaningful impact, there has to be a plan and a purpose to the plan and you have to diligently pursue it.

PLAN, PURPOSE AND PURSUIT

A plan is a method, program or scheme worked out beforehand for the accomplishment of an objective. God has an aim or objective in mind concerning your creation. This is why you are fearfully and wonderfully made. Your life is fitting into the divine plan.

> We are assured and know that [God being a partner in their labor] all things work together and are [fitting into a plan] for good to and for those who love God and are called according to [His] design and purpose. (Romans 8:28, TAB)

When Isaac was digging, he was not perturbed by all the accusations because God was a partner in his labor. All their accusations were working together to take him to his wide-open spaces. As they were accusing him, God was making room for him according to His design and purpose. The statement "And we know that God causes everything to work together" implies that God has a plan and is working towards the realization of that plan in our lives no matter what the situation seems like right now. The plan that God has in mind is intended for good. No matter the difficulty, disappointment or despondency that we might be facing, it does not change the fact that God is a good God. He wants us to be partakers of His divine nature. His divine nature is good. The scripture talks about His goodness:

> Praise ye the LORD. O give thanks unto the LORD; for he
> is good: for his mercy endureth for ever.
> (Psalm 106:1, KJV)

> O give thanks unto the LORD, for he is good: for his mercy
> endureth for ever. (Psalm 107:1, KJV)

> Oh that men would praise the LORD for his goodness, and
> for his wonderful works to the children of men!
> (Psalm 107:8, KJV)

God is "more good" than any friend or foe. His goodness cannot
be compared to that of an earthly parent, brother, sister, relative,
colleague, CEO, boss, bishop, deacon or pastor.

> When my father and my mother forsake me, then the LORD
> will take me up. (Psalm 27:10, KJV)

> Can a woman forget her sucking child, that she should not
> have compassion on the son of her womb? yea, they may
> forget, yet will I not forget thee. (Isaiah 49:15, KJV)

When parents abandon or disown you and friends say they do
not want to have anything to do with you, the good nature of
God shows up, He will then dust you up, clean you up and
propel you to the next dimension in kingdom excellence. It is
because of His goodness that He created man in His own image
and He empowered man to be fruitful, multiply, replenish and
subdue. When He anointed His only begotten son, an attribute
that He gave him was the empowerment to do good.

> How God anointed Jesus of Nazareth with the Holy Ghost
> and with power: who went about doing good, and healing

all that were oppressed of the devil; for God was with him. (Acts 10:38, KJV)

Because of Gods inherent good nature, every part of him seeks or plans to do good unto man.

> For I know the plans I have for you," says the LORD. "They are plans for good and not for disaster, to give you a future and a hope. (Jeremiah 29:11, NLT)

For each and every one of us, God has a unique plan and His plan for you is for distinction, not disaster. You are not a disaster waiting to happen but a diadem waiting to be adorned. A reason why we go through challenges and difficulties is due to the familiarity that used to exist between Lucifer and God. When an individual spends time in another person's home, he will know a little about that individual. It is the little that Satan knows that he is trying to use against the people of God. The Word of God tells us that Satan (Lucifer) used to live in Gods abode and even had access to His holy mountain.

> You were in Eden, the garden of God. I ordained and anointed you as the mighty angelic guardian. You had access to the holy mountain of God and walked among the stones of fire. (Ezekiel 28:13–14, NLT)

The knowledge that Lucifer gained about God is that God is a good God and the primary desire of God is to do good. Because of this knowledge, Satan is always devising plans to thwart the goodness of God in your life. I pray that Satan will continue to fail concerning you in Jesus' name. When Satan looks at you, knowing fully well that you are an heir of the father and a joint heir with the son, he automatically realizes that a program has been written concerning your life and that the code and the logic of the code is to result in "good" when executed. Satan also knows that there are some if, when and where clauses in the code statement. He tries to introduce bugs into the code so that the execution of the program, instead of resulting in good, turns to an error—demonic plan.

DEMONIC PLANS / Tactics

Satan has a plan but it is the counsel of God that shall stand.

> He frustrates the plans of the crafty, so their efforts will not succeed. (Job 5:12, NLT)

One way that Satan uses to carry out his plan is *obedience*. You are a slave to whoever you obey. If you obey Satan and his evil schemes, you become a slave to him. It is either you obey the law of the spirit of life or that of sin and death. In the book of Exodus, you see the plan of Satan to destroy the male children; in other words, the future.

> Then Pharaoh, the king of Egypt, gave this order to the Hebrew midwives, Shiphrah and Puah: "When you help the Hebrew women give birth, kill all the boys as soon as they are born. Allow only the baby girls to live." But because the midwives feared God, they refused to obey the king and allowed the boys to live, too. Then the king called for the midwives. "Why have you done this?" he demanded. "Why have you allowed the boys to live?" "Sir," they told him, "the Hebrew women are very strong. They have their babies so quickly that we cannot get there in time! They are not slow in giving birth like Egyptian women.
> (Exodus 1:15–19, NLT)

The Hebrew women refused to obey the king of Egypt. Instead of killing the babies, God gave them wisdom to give the right answer to the king of Egypt. We have to be careful not to obey the lies of Satan. Obeying God always comes with a price but God always reward those that are faithful to Him because if you are willing and obedient you will eat the good of the land. Satan never gives something without taking anything back. For anything you get from him, you have to pay a lot back. It is only the blessing of the Lord that makes rich and He adds no sorrow to it. You always become a slave to what you obey. The servants of Abimelech were trying to frustrate the future of Isaac. They did not realize that they were working according to a demonic plan. The same God that frustrated the plan of Pharaoh of Egypt frustrated the plan of Abimelech's servant. He is the still the same and He will frustrate every frustrater in your life in Jesus' name, Amen. God has a way of preparing "midwives" to see to the birth of your greatness.

Satan also uses *humiliation* to achieve His plan so much so that you begin to cry, "Look at what has befallen me." In the book of Esther, Haman constantly humiliated Mordecai at the gate because he did not bow down for him. He was not satisfied with this. He then extended the humiliation to destruction of Mordecai and his people but God decided to humiliate Haman in return.

> When Haman told his wife, Zeresh, and all his friends what had happened, they said, "Since Mordecai—this man who has humiliated you—is a Jew, you will never succeed in your plans against him. It will be fatal to continue to oppose him. (Esther 6:13, NLT)

Another way that Satan uses to carry out his plan is *neglect*. He makes sure you are sidetracked. You begin to doubt yourself and even think something is wrong with you. If I could be pushed aside then I must really be worthless. I am only good for the wilderness or jungle. The good news is that the eyes of the Lord go to and fro. It does not matter where you are, God can locate you.

> Then he asked Jesse, "Is this it? Are there no more sons?"
> "Well, yes, there's the runt. But he's out tending the sheep."
> Samuel ordered Jesse, "Go get him. We're not moving from
> this spot until he's here. (1 Samuel 16:11, MSG)

DIVINE PLAN

Despite the constant failures of Satan, he is always making plans but in all his plans, God is always ahead of him. God is following His plan for your life and only He knows it; Satan does not. The Word of God declares in the book of Jeremiah, "For I know the plans," not "we" know the plan. No matter how much Satan schemes by throwing disease, discouragement and despondency your way, he is only playing games. Satan does not know.

> God is able to make you strong, just as the Good News says. It is the message about Jesus Christ and his plan for you Gentiles, a plan kept secret from the beginning of time. (Romans 16:25, NLT)

Since it is a plan for you, you need to thirst for it. You need to ask for it, knock on it and seek for it. His plan for you is a divine plan, not a demonic one. One of the reasons why we sometimes ask questions like, "God what are you doing, how are things like this?" is because we do not understand the plan of God for us in detail, and hence we miss opportunities. Thomas Edison, said, "Opportunity is missed by most people because it is dressed in overalls and looks like work."

Joshua was a man that God gave a wonderful promise to but he still needed a plan of action. Despite the fact that he was able to cross the Jordan when it overflows its bank and the inhabitants of Jericho were scared, He still sought for the divine plan. As Christians, though we pray and fast, we should also desire a step-by-step schedule of action.

> I know what I am doing. I have it all planned out–plans to take care of you, not abandon you. Plans to give you the future you hope for. (Jeremiah 29:11, MSG)

God has got you all planned out in detail. A glorious revelation is that he knows what is best for you and this is the reason why he is able to make what you hope for correspond with his divine plan for you.

To live a fruitful, flourishing and fulfilling life, you need the divine plan. There is a plan, and the plan. A plan is what you get for different occasions. This can also be referred to as the sub plan. When you look at an architect that has drawn the plan for a building, there will be lots of rooms and other structures in the building. The whole drawing of the building is the plan, while that of the rooms or other structures can be called the sub-plan. The plan is the blue print of God for your life. It will be detailed, and it will take you from where you are to where you ought to be. It will also ensure that you do not dabble into what you ought not to do. This is because every one of your steps is being divinely ordered according to the divine plan.

WHY WE NEED THE DIVINE PLAN

Man cannot make good plans.

> I know, LORD, that a person's life is not his own. No one is able to plan his own course. (Jeremiah 10:23, NLT)

You cannot plan the course, route or path of your life. It is only God that can guarantee smooth sailing. Jonah was given specific instructions according to the Divine plan of God to proceed to Nineveh; instead he fled to Tarshish. On the way, the ship he was traveling in encountered a fierce storm. He had to be thrown overboard. He did not get to Tarshish. Man's plan at best is manageable but Gods plan is perfect. This is because He made all things. He can make the inanimate fit into the animate.

> You know me inside and out, you know every bone in my body; You know exactly how I was made, bit by bit, how I was sculpted from nothing into something. Like an open book, you watched me grow from conception to birth; all the stages of my life were spread out before you. The days of my life all prepared before I'd even lived one day.
> (Psalm 139: 15–16, MSG)

Sometimes we try to make our plans fit into situations or vice versa. When our plans become a colossal failure, we then wonder what we have done wrong. It then becomes a situation of "Had I known..." The Most High, being a perfect God, knows what is best for you. When it seems as if certain things are not making sense, he sure knows what he is doing.

"The heart has reasons that the head knows nothing of."

~Blaise Pascal

His plan is better than man's plan.

> "This "foolish" plan of God is far wiser than the wisest of human plans, and God's weakness is far stronger than the greatest of human strength."(1 Corinthians 1: 25, NLT)

A peculiar nature of Gods plan is that it never looks good to the wise. When you start acting on the plan, it is always at a time when what you are doing and the purpose of what you are doing seems like a mirage. When Noah was given an instruction to build an ark because of the impending doom looming over the earth, everybody around thought he had taken leave of his senses. At that time there had been no record of rain. The account of what looked like rain in the Bible then was water coming from the ground to water the earth. Now here comes the "web spinner."—Noah saying, "something called rain will fall. It will come from heaven, and the effect will be so great that everywhere will be destroyed except you are in something called the ark." Let us face reality; some of us will even doubt it this day. The plan of God always looks foolish.

Just like Jehoshaphat was told to prepare worshippers for battle, Joshua was told to march round the wall of Jericho, and Gideon was told to select 300 men that lapped the water. His plan may look foolish, but He is always right.

His plan is right.

> When they heard this, all the people, including the unjust
> tax collectors, agreed that God's plan was right.
> (Luke 7: 29, NLT)

Since He is the creator of all, and nothing was created without His knowledge, it follows that His plan will always be right. He does not have the capability to speak a lie. When Satan deceived Eve in the Garden of Eden, God pronounced that the seed from woman shall bruise the head of the serpent. By the time Jesus came lowly in a manger, was persecuted, nailed to the cross, and eventually died, Satan thought the plan had failed but the plan of God was right. Jesus, by His death, went and took the keys of hell and death from Satan. This was a great surprise to Satan.

His plan will come to pass.

> I will never abandon the descendants of Jacob or David, my
> servant, or change the plan that David's descendants will

rule the descendants of Abraham, Isaac, and Jacob. Instead, I will restore them to their land and have mercy on them. (Jeremiah 33:26 , NLT)

Any plan of God must definitely come to pass. His plan is His word. The Word of God is yea and Amen. Forever the Word of God is settled. Whatever plan God makes will definitely happen. God told a woman called Rebecca that she had two nations in her womb and that the elder will serve the younger. Esau (the Edomites) ended up serving Jacob (the Israelites). God is watching over His plan to make sure it comes to fulfillment (Jeremiah 1:12)

He is a partner in the plan.

We are assured and know that [God being a partner in their labor] all things work together and are [fitting into a plan] for good to and for those who love God and are called according to [His] design and purpose. (Romans 8: 28, **TAB**)

No matter the amount of money that any company has, the strength of the company lies in the human personnel. They will devise the policies, chart the course and execute any plan. In some cases the plan or policy could be excellent but execution may be sub-par. With God as a partner in any plan, there is no question about the accuracy or effectiveness of the plan. God works both to will and do of his good pleasure. He is able to time everything to work together for good.

To know what to pray for.

Go ahead, examine me from inside out, surprise me in the middle of the night—You'll find I'm just what I say I am. My words don't run loose. (Psalm 17:3, **MSG**)

Elijah was able to declare to Ahab that there will be no rain because of an understanding of God's divine plan (1 Kings 17:1). An understanding of the Word of God concerning any situation reveals His mind or plan, and this ensures that you do not pray amiss. In the words of the psalmist, he said "my words do not run loose." You are able to pray with pin-point accuracy. Your prayer becomes effectual.

It can withstand adversity.

My soul is escaped out of the snare of the fowler."
(Psalms 124:7, KJV)

The plan of God can withstand any adversity or adversary. The Word of God talks about the accuser of brethren in the book of Revelation and how he was overcome—through the blood of the lamb and the word of testimony. The plan of God is infallible. At a time, John the beloved, the writer of Revelation, was shown the vision of a book and there was nobody available to open the book. He was distraught, but later on he was told to stop crying, that the lion of the tribe of Judah had opened the book, and also broken the seal. God is always ahead of any adversary; that is why His plan will always withstand any adversity. When Noah built an ark according to the plan of God, the floods could not penetrate. All that were in the ark came out alive, while those that did not enter perished.

It is blessed.

A blessing is a command or summons to all the forces in the universe to assist someone. When Divinity designs a plan, all the forces in the universe have no choice other than to assist the manifestation of the plan. When God decided that Jonah should go to Nineveh, and he was going to Tarshish, the sea cooperated with God to bring about a storm. Not only did the sea cooperate, but also a whale provided accommodation for Jonah.

THE PLAN WAS PUT TOGETHER BY THE TRINITY

It is drafted by the Trinity.

> God said, Let Us [Father, Son, and Holy Spirit] make mankind in Our image, after Our likeness, and let them have complete authority over the fish of the sea, the birds of the air, the [tame] beasts, and over all of the earth, and over everything that creeps upon the earth. (Genesis 1:26, **TAB**)

God the Father is the head of the plan.

> Yours, O LORD , is the greatness and the power and the glory and the majesty and the splendor, for everything in heaven and earth is yours. Yours, O LORD, is the kingdom; you are exalted as head over all. (1 Chronicle 29:11, **TAB**)

God the son is the chief architect of the plan.

> For it was in Him that all things were created, in heaven and on earth, things seen and things unseen, whether thrones, dominions, rulers, or authorities; all things were created and exist through Him [by His service, intervention] and in and for Him. (Collosians 1:16, **TAB**)

God the Holy spirit executes the plan.

> The earth was without form and an empty waste, and darkness was upon the face of the very great deep. The Spirit of God was moving (hovering, brooding) over the face of the waters. (Gen 1:2, **TAB**)

At this point, with all the wonderful attributes of the plan, you should be panting for the plan as the deer pants for the water brooks.

HOW TO GET THE PLAN

As Joshua approached the city of Jericho, he looked up and saw a man facing him with sword in hand. Joshua went up to him and asked, "Are you friend or foe?" "Neither one," he replied. "I am commander of the LORD's army." At this, Joshua fell with his face to the ground in reverence. "I am at your command," Joshua said. "What do you want your servant to do?" The commander of the LORD's army replied, "Take off your sandals, for this is holy ground." And Joshua did as he was told. (Joshua 5: 13 - 15, NLT)

Joshua the servant of Moses was a man saddled with a big task—leading the Israelites to the Promised Land, a land flowing with milk and honey. He was aware of all that his predecessor went through. He realized that this was a huge responsibility. The only way to achieve good success would be by leaning on the everlasting arm.

In any venture, it is only by leaning on the everlasting arms that we can succeed. For the joy of the Lord is our strength, in Jesus' name. Joshua was a man greatly helped by the Lord. When he received the mantle from Moses, he was encouraged by the people and by God. He was a man in motion. He started moving according to divine instruction. He passed over Jordan at the time the river overflowed its bank. The people living in Canaan (Promised Land) were afraid on hearing about this.

Now when all the Amorite kings west of the Jordan and all the Canaanite kings along the coast heard how the LORD had dried up the Jordan before the Israelites until we had

crossed over, their hearts melted and they no longer had the
courage to face the Israelites. (Joshua 5: 1, NIV)

At this point in the lives of Joshua and the Israelites, they were
at the fringe of Canaan. They tasted of the fruit of Canaan, they
had a change of diet, they took over storehouses that they did
not build, but their eyes did not shift from the objective. They
desired the divine plan to take over Jericho—a city of palm trees.
In our lives, there is the divine plan that will lift us from penury
to prosperity and from breakdown to breakthrough. To get the
plan you must:

PRAY

...he looked up and saw... (Joshua 5:13, NLT)

Prayer is a catch 22. To get the plan, you need to pray; when you
get the plan, you need to pray. A master key is prayer. It is the
secret of power with God. Irrespective of your status or spiritual
level, you need to pray.

And in the morning, rising up a great while before day,
he went out, and departed into a solitary place, and there
prayed. (Mark 1:35, NLT)

Prayer involves separation. There is collective and individual
prayer. Prayer is a time when there is mutual communication between God and man. During prayer, you bare your mind without holding back. An energy sapping aspect of a Christian life is
prayer. It involves dedication, diligence, perseverance and purity.
Between the time that Joshua looked up and the time he "saw,"
lots of effort would have been put in.

Confess your faults one to another, and pray one for another, that ye may be healed. The effectual fervent prayer of a righteous man availeth much. (James 5: 16, KJV)

The word "effectual" means sufficient or adequate to produce a result, while "fervent" means intense. Our prayer has to be intense for the desired result. You have to create time and do it. You pray to live and live to pray. You pray until something happens.

And Elijah said unto Ahab, Get thee up, eat and drink; for there is a sound of abundance of rain. So Ahab went up to eat and to drink. And Elijah went up to the top of Carmel; and he cast himself down upon the earth, and put his face between his knees, And said to his servant, Go up now, look toward the sea. And he went up, and looked, and said, There is nothing. And he said, Go again seven times. And it came to pass at the seventh time, that he said, Behold, there ariseth a little cloud out of the sea, like a man's hand. And he said, Go up, say unto Ahab, Prepare thy chariot, and get thee down that the rain stop thee not.
(1 Kings 18: 41 - 44, KJV)

Elijah told Ahab to go and eat while he was fasting and praying. This involved self-sacrifice and control. When Joshua decided to look up, he was dedicated to looking up. Looking up means lifting up ones eyes to the Lord without distraction. When we start to pray, sometimes we begin on a particular point and before we know it, we would have veered into something else. In some cases, for want of nothing to say, we keep on repeating the same thing. When we get distracted while praying, the focus is lost. Do not lose focus while praying, for prayer wipes away sadness and shame.

Lord may this family to pass the test of destiny! Lord

Those who look to him for help will be radiant with joy; no shadow of shame will darken their faces. I cried out to the lord in my suffering, and he heard me. He set me free from all my fears. (Psalm 34:5–6, NLT)

You have to know the word for your prayer to be effective. When you begin to pray and some things starts to drop into your spirit man, it is your knowledge of the word that will allow you to sift the wheat from the chaff. It is the Word of God that will act as the litmus test.

By your words I can see where I'm going; they throw a beam of light on my dark path. (Psalm 119:105, msg)

PROCEED

...And Joshua went up to him. (Joshua 5: 13, NLT)

To proceed means to go forward in an orderly manner. It means to follow a certain course. Joshua saw a man, but he was not sure who he was. Despite this uncertainty, Joshua moved towards him. When you are trying to get the Divine plan, you keep on going forward. If you have earmarked 30 days to fast, you continue. Anything else other than this is double-mindedness. You are telling God that you have laid it all on His altar; there is no going back.

Ask boldly, believingly, without a second thought. People who "worry their prayers" are like wind-whipped waves. (James 1: 6, MSG)

It is when you proceed that you progress.

Elisha then returned to his oxen, killed them, and used the wood from the plow to build a fire to roast their flesh. He passed around the meat to the other plowmen, and they all ate. Then he went with Elijah as his assistant.

(1 Kings 19: 21, NLT)

By this action, Elisha made sure that he displayed to God, to man, to himself and even to the devil that he is not going back to the old business. He is now involved with a new business partner. This partner can sometimes be a cattle farmer, a dealer in precious gems, a medical doctor, an adviser, a treasurer, etc. When you proceed, you are not staying in your comfort zone. You can no longer rely on the predictable to achieve excellence. Woe to him that is at ease in Zion.

> In a time of drastic change it is the learners who inherit the future. The learned usually find themselves equipped to live in a world that no longer exists.
>
> -Eric Hoffer (1902–1983).

Proceeding implies an ability to change. Albert Einstein said, "everything has changed, but the people have not changed."

PERSIST

...Are you friend or foe. (Joshua 5: 13, NLT)

Your persistence will prevent you from making wrong assumptions. Most of the terrible mistakes we have made in life are due to wrong assumptions. Because it looks like what we want does not mean that it is the real thing. After the death of Amnon and Absalom, Adonijah was the heir apparent to the throne of the king of Israel when David dies. Adonijah, before the death of David, started parading himself as king; he even got some of

David's advisers to join his camp. At the end of the day he was rejected, and he died unceremoniously. Do not jump to a hasty conclusion. Make your calling and election sure. If Paul can say "that I may know him" and that he presses forward towards the mark of the high calling, you cannot afford to "kill time" with inactivity.

I have been to some interviews or answered some questionnaires where the questions looked repetitive. The aim of the interviewer is to get a pattern and make sure that the right candidate will be selected. In persisting you want to make sure you get the plan.

If you fail to persist you will fail to prevail.

> When Elisha was in his last illness, King Jehoash of Israel visited him and wept over him. "My father! My father! The chariots and charioteers of Israel!" he cried. Elisha told him, "Get a bow and some arrows." And the king did as he was told. Then Elisha told the king of Israel to put his hand on the bow, and Elisha laid his own hands on the king's hands. Then he commanded, "Open that eastern window," and he opened it. Then he said, "Shoot!" So he did. Then Elisha proclaimed, "This is the LORD's arrow, full of victory over Aram, for you will completely conquer the Arameans at Aphek. Now pick up the other arrows and strike them against the ground." So the king picked them up and struck the ground three times. But the man of God was angry with him. "You should have struck the ground five or six times!" he exclaimed. "Then you would have beaten Aram until they were entirely destroyed. Now you will be victorious only three times. (2 Kings 13:14–19, NLT)

Compare the response of Jehoash King of Israel with that of Jacob in a wrestling bout with a man until the daybreak. When the man saw that he was not winning, he dislocated Jacob's thigh, thinking that will dissuade Jacob, but Jacob did not give up. Jacob was dogged.

> Then the man said, "Let me go, for it is dawn. " But Jacob panted, "I will not let you go unless you bless me.
> (Genesis 32: 26, NLT)

PRAISE

> ...Joshua fell with his face to the ground.
> (Joshua 5: 14, NLT)

The term "fell to the ground" does not represent an anatomical posture but honor and submission. Reverence him. When you want something you have never had, you have to do something you have never done. Sometimes we make the mistake of leaving our cell phone on when we want to pray, most especially pastors and ministers because somebody in need could call. Since when do we have the ability to heal or deliver?

> *If you want to be up to date with what is happening in the ter-restrial, you will be obsolete when it comes to celestial matters.*

> But the time is coming and is already here when true worshipers will worship the Father in spirit and in truth. The Father is looking for anyone who will worship him that way. For God is Spirit, so those who worship him must worship in spirit and in truth. (John 4: 23–24, NLT)

PREPARE

> ...Take off your sandals. (Joshua 5: 15, NLT)

Elijah told Ahab to go and rejoice before the rain came. Eli told Hannah that she would have a child by the next festival, and she believed the Word of God.

> And she said, Let thine handmaid find grace in thy sight. So the woman went her way, and did eat, and her countenance was no more sad. (1 Samuel 1: 18, KJV)

The woman was yet to physically receive the promise, but she changed her outlook. Her countenance changed to that of somebody expectant and God was true to his word. Your preparation for that which is expected will ensure that you call those things that be not as though they were. When you are about to have a guest, you prepare for the guest. When you prepare for the plan, you forsake those things that can cause the plan to be delayed or denied.

> Then said Jesus unto his disciples, If any man will come after me, let him deny himself, and take up his cross, and follow me. (Matthew 16:24, KJV)

> Therefore, since we are surrounded by such a huge crowd of witnesses to the life of faith, let us strip off every weight that slows us down, especially the sin that so easily hinders our progress. And let us run with endurance the race that God has set before us. (Hebrew 12:1, NLT)

HOW TO KNOW YOU HAVE THE PLAN

It consumes

> When I heard these things, I sat down and wept. For some days I mourned and fasted and prayed before the God of heaven. Then I said: "O LORD , God of heaven, the great and awesome God, who keeps his covenant of love with those who love him and obey his commands,

(Nehemiah 1:4–5, NIV)

When you get the plan, you are not able to rest until you do the bidding of God. Where you are no longer agrees with what you saw; therefore there is a thirst to achieve what you saw. The psalmist said "the zeal of the house of the Lord has consumed me." You are not dissuaded by whatever may come your way. Ruth got the plan and she was able to tell Naomi that "your God will be my God and your people will be my people."

It confronts

When Sanballat the Horonite and Tobiah the Ammonite official heard about this, they were very much disturbed that someone had come to promote the welfare of the Israelites. (Nehemiah 2:10, NIV)

The plan confronts every adversary. When the shepherds saw the star and they started following the star to lead them to Jesus, at a point in time they came across Herod. Herod, on learning of the mission of the shepherds, was disturbed and distressed. He wanted to know where baby Jesus was laid so that he could do him harm. Herod did not succeed in this scheme. He was eventually consumed by worms the same day that he died. Another example was during the birth of Moses, when Pharaoh commanded the midwives to kill all the male children born to the Jews. When the adversaries see that you have the plan, their peace is gone. In your place of work, when you begin to take the right steps and make "informed decisions" (based on knowledge from the throne of grace), some of your colleagues will not be happy because they know you are on an upward march.

It challenges

There, by the Ahava Canal, I proclaimed a fast, so that we might humble ourselves before our God and ask him for a safe journey for us and our children, with all our possessions. I was ashamed to ask the king for soldiers and horsemen to protect us from enemies on the road, because we had told the king, "The gracious hand of our God is on everyone who looks to him, but his great anger is against all who forsake him." So we fasted and petitioned our God about this, and he answered our prayer. (Ezra 8:21–23, NIV)

When you get the divine plan, you are challenged to move from mediocrity to excellence. You have a burning desire to do all it takes. What others regard as obstacles, you see as opportunities, and what is referred to as setbacks is taken as a steppingstone. There is a willingness to take on tasks that others run away from. They that know their God shall be strong and then do exploits. You realize that you are destined to do exploits because you know what others do not know.

From that day on, half of my men did the work, while the other half were equipped with spears, shields, bows and armor. Neither I nor my brothers nor my men nor the guards with me took off our clothes; each had his weapon, even when he went for water. (Nehemiah 4: 16, 23, NIV)

It connects—- (with power and personnel)

And may I have a letter to Asaph, keeper of the king's forest, so he will give me timber to make beams for the gates of the citadel by the temple and for the city wall and for the residence I will occupy?" And because the gracious hand of my God was upon me, the king granted my requests. So I went to the governors of Trans-Euphrates and gave them the king's letters. The king had also sent army officers and cavalry with me. (Nehemiah 2:8–9, NIV)

Where there is vision, God always makes a provision. When you have the divine plan for your life, it may take time, but you will ultimately be connected to vision helpers. When David became king and Hiram king of Tyre came to visit him with numerous gifts, David said he perceived that God has decided to establish his kingdom. God will always establish the kingdom of the king that has the divine plan. You are no exception. As a king, all you need to do is get the divine plan for your life and God will make your feet like hinds feet so that you will be able to get to your high places, and also walk upon your high places.

God is bound by His word and the plan from him still seeks to connect (see John 3:16, Numbers 10:29, Zechariah 8:23, Acts 15:18).

It crushes

> When all our enemies heard about this, all the surrounding nations were afraid and lost their self-confidence, because they realized that this work had been done with the help of our God. (Nehemiah 6:16, NIV)

The divine plan crushes every resistance. When the Apostles were arrested and were brought in for trial, despite the fact that they were not learned, they spoke with boldness. They said, "We ought to obey God rather than men." The arresters were cut to the heart by their response and reference to Jesus. They decided to slay them. One of them called Gamaliel then gave a wise counsel:

> But one member had a different perspective. He was a Pharisee named Gamaliel, who was an expert on religious law and was very popular with the people. He stood up and ordered that the apostles be sent outside the council chamber for a while. Then he addressed his colleagues as follows: "Men of Israel, take care what you are planning to do to these

men! Some time ago there was that fellow Theudas, who pretended to be someone great. About four hundred others joined him, but he was killed, and his followers went their various ways. The whole movement came to nothing. After him, at the time of the census, there was Judas of Galilee. He got some people to follow him, but he was killed, too, and all his followers were scattered. "So my advice is, leave these men alone. If they are teaching and doing these things merely on their own, it will soon be overthrown. But if it is of God, you will not be able to stop them. You may even find yourselves fighting against God." The council accepted his advice. (Acts 5: 34 -40 NLT)

Every resistance to the plan of God in your life shall be crushed in Jesus' name, amen.

It consecrates

No one is greater in this house than I am. My master has withheld nothing from me except you, because you are his wife. How then could I do such a wicked thing and sin against God? (Genesis 39:9, NIV)

When you get the divine plan, you become set apart. Since you are focused on the plan, it is easy to live a holy life. Joseph was not prepared to involve himself in adultery because he understood that there is a plan written about his life that must be fulfilled.

It controls

But David said to Abishai, "Don't destroy him! Who can lay a hand on the LORD's anointed and be guiltless? As surely as the LORD lives," he said, "the LORD himself will strike him; either his time will come and he will die, or he will go

into battle and perish. But the LORD forbid that I should lay a hand on the LORD's anointed. Now get the spear and water jug that are near his head, and let's go.
(1 Samuel 26:9–11, NIV)

With the divine plan, your emotions and temperament are controlled. David simply said, "who can lay his hand on the anointed of God and be guiltless." Things that you would normally do that are lawful become a taboo to you because they are not right.

THE PURSUIT

You are a part of the glorious plan of the Most High God. In any plan, the purpose is for the plan to glorify the name of the Lord.

The people I made especially for myself, a people custom-made to praise me. (Isaiah 43: 21, MSG)

As a custom made being, you have been carefully crafted. God put lots of effort and time in creating a special you. He created you with a purpose in mind—for you to fit into the plan. The plan is a means of attaining an objective. The plan of God as it is unfolding in your life right now may be wrapped in adversity, but it will ultimately lead to adoration. You may be in a dungeon; you will eventually wear a diadem. It may be fraught with trials, but you will testify in Jesus' name.

The pursuit of the plan to achieve the purpose is the difference between fulfilling the purpose and failing the purpose. The way we pursue the plan is more important to God than the purpose.

A soldier on duty doesn't get caught up in making deals at the marketplace. He concentrates on carrying out orders. An athlete who refuses to play by the rules will never get anywhere. (2 Timothy 2:4–5, MSG)

Follow the Lord's rules for doing his work, just as an athlete either follows the rules or is disqualified and wins no prize. (2 Timothy 2:5, NLT)

For every plan there are rules. Flouting the rule leads to failure. Deviating from the rules leads to disqualification. As an athlete in a 100 meter sprint cannot cross the line during the course of the race. You also must obey all the rules in the pursuit of the plan. Specific instructions were given to Joshua in the plan to take over Jericho and he followed them to the letter. March around the city once every day for six days, and on the seventh day, march around the city seven times. Seven priests were expected to bear seven trumpets. It is not anybody that can bear the trumpets. There would be lots of people that were more skilled in blowing the trumpets but the instruction says priests should blow the trumpets. The trumpets were also not any kind of trumpet. They were to be made with ram's horns; not silver, brass or gold.

For the first six days the trumpet must not be blown except on the seventh day, after which the people were expected to shout. The shout must be on the seventh day after the trumpet had been blown. Then something will happen. *The plan of God may be shrouded in mystery. Proper pursuit will determine if it will result in misery, or merrymaking.* In Luke chapter 5, Jesus met a man by the name of Peter. Before meeting the man at all, He already had a purpose for him—to be a fisher of men. Jesus now put a plan in place and Peter started pursuing the plan. An instruction was given to Peter to "let down his nets." In the pursuit of the plan, God is telling some of us to let down our nets, which, according to Pastor E. A. Adeboye, could mean:

You have tried before, but try again
Be ready for hard work
Do not lose hope
Trust in me
Do what you have never done before
In most cases, we do as Peter did:

> And Simon answering said unto him, Master, we have toiled all the night, and have taken nothing: nevertheless at thy word I will let down the net. (Luke 5: 5, KJV)

Peter only let down one net instead of all the nets. Peter caught lots of fish but what he could have caught cannot be compared to what he caught.

Myopic pursuit leads to the celebration of mediocrity in place of excellence.

HOW TO PURSUE

Without Division

God told David to pursue, overtake and he will without fail recover all. He did exactly what God said. One thing that is not contestable or debatable is a decision that God has made before you gave your life to him that He would help you. And he is ready to help you right early, but you need a face set like a flint, determined to do his will.

> Because the Sovereign LORD helps me, I will not be dismayed. Therefore, I have set my face like a stone, determined to do his will. And I know that I will triumph.
> (Isaiah 50:7, NLT)

Purpose minus Focus = Failure

Dreams inspire, visions guide and values sustain. In the pursuit of the plan, the desire must be for His will to be fulfilled. There is no limit to how God can do it. Because He did something for an individual in a certain way does not mean that is the way He is going to do it for you. Pursue what He has mentioned to you without division. Jeremiah said he found the Word of God and he ate the word, and it became a joy and rejoicing to his soul. Use the Word of God according to the right dose; do not copy another person. Two people can go to the doctor with the same symptom, and subsequently get the same diagnosis. The doctor may prescribe the same medication, but the dosage may differ based on individual constitution or threshold. If Individual A decides to copy the dosage of B, it is likely to be disastrous.

Without Distress

You cannot make informed decision when in distress. When David came to Ziklag and his family and friends were nowhere to be found, he was in distress, and he could not pursue. When in distress, you are unable to think straight. Your mind will be clouded with worry. This is the reason why God always encourage us to "fear not."

> Samuel said to Saul, "Why have you disturbed me by bringing me up?" "I am in great distress," Saul said. "The Philistines are fighting against me, and God has turned away from me. He no longer answers me, either by prophets or by dreams. So I have called on you to tell me what to do.
> (1 Samuel 28: 15, **NIV**)

Distress plus Decision = Disaster

Pursue the plan with enthusiasm. Ralph Waldo Emerson said, "Every great and commanding moment in the annals of the world is the triumph of some enthusiasm."

Therefore with joy shall ye draw water out of the wells of salvation. (Isaiah 12:3, KJV)

If you look at a typical well (for those that has lived in a developing nation before), there has to be an amount of joy for you to draw water out of it. If you are in distress, you will not be composed to draw the water from the well. This could result in the following: the water will be full of impurities, the bucket will not be full, the vessel used in drawing the water can fall inside the well, the person drawing the water can fall inside the well and you will spend more time trying to fill the bucket.

Without Delay

If you miss the time to make a decision, you miss your season to shine. *Season missed is success sacrificed.* In any endeavor, time is of essence. The Lord is your shepherd when you work according to time. Do not be a procrastinator. What you can do now, do not leave until later. Pursue as if today is the last day. Remember the story of the rich fool? He was planning for tomorrow but God said today he will give account. All that you need to do, do it quickly.

> For he saith, I have heard thee in a time accepted, and in the day of salvation have I succoured thee: behold, now is the accepted time; behold, now is the day of salvation.
> (2 Corinthians 6:2, KJV)

Remember, "now" is the accepted time.

Without Deceit

God knows both the deceiver and the deceived. There is nothing hidden from Him. If you are pursuing a divine plan, it has to be done truthfully. You cannot deceive Him even though you succeed in deceiving men. If you strive for masteries, do it lawfully.

You must not belong to the camp that says, "the end justifies the means" or "I do not care whose ox is gored." If you do not care, the owner of the plan (i.e. God) cares.

After Elisha gave instructions to Naaman of Syria on what he needed to do to be healed from leprosy, Elisha did not receive anything from him. This did not please Gehazi, the servant of Elisha. Gehazi ran after Naaman, collected gifts from him, and ran back to Elisha. He then lied to Elisha, forgetting that the eyes of the Lord go to and fro to see whose heart is right with him. Deceit can bring leprosy.

> He went in and stood before his master. Elisha said, Where have you been, Gehazi? He said, Your servant went nowhere. Elisha said to him, Did not my spirit go with you when the man turned from his chariot to meet you? Was it a time to accept money, garments, olive orchards, vineyards, sheep, oxen, menservants, and maidservants? Therefore the leprosy of Naaman shall cleave to you and to your offspring forever. And Gehazi went from his presence a leper as white as snow. (2 Kings 5:25–27, **TAB**)

Without Doubt

> The commander of the **LORD**'s army replied, "Take off your sandals, for this is holy ground." And Joshua did as he was told. (Joshua 5:15, **NLT**)

Joshua did as he was told to get the plan. He did not doubt the Word of God. Since he did not doubt the plan, he was wholly committed to the pursuit of the plan. For you to achieve results, you must not be of two minds. When the man sick with palsy in the Bible was taken to the roof by his friends, he agreed with them. They were in one accord.

NUGGETS

- Success does not happen by accident; it is always by design.
- Excellence will always silence detractors.
- With impact you stand out, and without it you blend in.
- The hypostasis of impact is input.
- God has a unique plan for each one of us, and His plan is for distinction and not disaster.
- The plan is the blue print of God for your life.
- To God, the way we pursue the plan is more important than the purpose.
- You become a slave of whom you choose to obey.
- The key success factors to achieving your plan are to: pray; proceed; persist; praise; prepare.
- Prayer is the master key to victory. It is the secret of power with God. Prayer wipes away sadness and shame.

PRAYER POINTS

- Father, make me a person of impact, in Jesus' name.
- Let the "excellence of my greatness" make a strong and lasting impression on all around me.
- I refuse to allow controversy and mediocrity to hold me back, in Jesus' name.
- El-shaddai, in line with your plan, propel me to the next level in Kingdom excellence.
- The Lion of Judah, frustrate every counsel of Satan and his demons against me; let only your counsel stand in my life, in Jesus' name.
- Oh Lord, I know that your plan is better than my plan, right, and you alone can bring it to pass. Lord, establish your plan of greatness in my life in Jesus' name.
- My Lord, I know your plan for me can withstand any adversity, let your plans for my greatness be fulfilled now, in Jesus' name.
- The Great I AM, give me focus in the place of prayer, that I may receive your plan.
- The Unchanging Changer, give unto me the grace to persist and keep on moving in the plan in Jesus' name.
- Alpha and Omega, let your plan for greatness consume me. Let the plan be accomplished in Jesus' name.

YOUR BEST IS YET TO COME

We are at a time that has been aptly described as the *dispensation of grace*. It is a time that we who were before far away have been brought closer to enter into the holy of holies with boldness, in as much as we are undefiled, because whether at a time of grace or law, God still remains the same (though his presence in any situation causes the situation to defy every law imaginable to human comprehension). The word "dispensation" is a noun. It is taken from the verb dispense (action word) which means to deal out in parts, or portion or to prepare and give out. We are at a time when God is giving out what he had prepared. You may not have what you want in full; it is because God is giving it out in dosages, not because he has not prepared it. A good understanding of dispensation could be likened to a doctor that has a patient. Based on the symptoms and other laboratory tests, the doctor makes his diagnosis. He then prescribes a medication. The patient takes the prescription to the pharmacist, who then prepares the drug and the dosage. The patient is expected to take the medication based on the dosage. The whole of the medication will cause healing, but it is dispensed in dosages.

It is dispensed in dosages to prevent an overdose. What God had prepared can only be imagined. Even then it will still dwarf every imagination no matter the capacity for extravagance.

But on the contrary, as the Scripture says, What eye has not seen and ear has not heard and has not entered into the heart of man, [all that] God has prepared (made and keeps ready) for those who love Him [who hold Him in affectionate reverence, promptly obeying Him and gratefully recognizing the benefits He has bestowed]. (1Corinthians 2:9, TAB)

Dispensation could also mean to exempt or do away with. The old sin in all its ramifications (2 Corinthians 5:17) had to be discarded for the new to be able to purposefully operate. As we begin to function under the unction of the divine one in this dispensation, placing our feet in the path ordered by the holy one of Israel, there is elevation to a *dimension of establishment.* *"I know, God, that mere mortals can't run their own lives, That men and women don't have what it takes to take charge of life."* (Jeremiah 10:23, MSG)

This is a dimension of ability to do what you otherwise would not have been able to do. It is not as if you have not been established before you were born (Jeremiah 1:5) but a realization of what you have become (Acts 4:13; 1 Corinthians 15:10), by virtue of the acceptance of the gift of grace, now bestows knowledge. With knowledge comes a transformation in the thought process (Rom 12:2). Dimension of establishment implies following heavenly principles for promotion and progress. It involves relying on the whole Word of God, looking beyond the human sphere of physical visibility and comprehension. It could be as simple as "give, and it shall be given" or "sacrifice, and you shall be sanctified." The widow of Zarephath gave her last meal and many more meals were given to her while Abraham offered up Isaac as a sacrifice, and his generation was eternally sanctified. Dimension of establishment is a period of *obedience,* and its hypostasis is faith, faith in the truth—the truth that is described as *"Whom God hath raised up, having loosed the pains of death: because it was not possible that he should be holden of it"*(Acts 2:24, KJV). This is very comforting. Since it was not possible for death to hold Jesus from resurrecting, nothing can prevent you from becoming great except yourself.

The dimension of establishment is good, but where God is taking His children is far better than this. What will open the heavens for you to get to the next realm of abundance is obedience. Since dimension also means levels, and with every level there is at least a devil, there has to be *displacement of principalities*

> But everyone knows that you are obedient to the Lord. This makes me very happy. I want you to see clearly what is right and to stay innocent of any wrong. The God of peace will soon crush Satan under your feet. May the grace of our Lord Jesus Christ be with you."(Romans 16:19–20, NLT)

"Principality" simply means the governing authority over a region or the negative encroachment over your positive enlargement. These are forces that want to prevent you from breasting the tape of success and mounting the dais or platform of glory.

> Then the devil leaveth him, and, behold, angels came and ministered unto him. (Matthew 4:11, KJV)

Until the devil takes its leave from you, angels cannot truly minister to you.

> Send us into those pigs," the evil spirits begged. Jesus gave them permission. (Mark 5:12, NLT)

Until the evil spirits are sent into the herd of pigs, you may not come to your right mind.

With the displacement of principalities comes *distinction of power.* People suddenly notice that you are in existence. People may now flood you with questions like, "Where have you been" or "We never thought you could do this." Deep in your mind you are thinking, "I have been here all the time," or "This is the same mantra that I have been mouthing all the while." The difference is that your best is now beginning to appear but it is still not your best because no eye has seen nor ear heard; neither has the mind conceived what God has prepared to do in your life. What you have attained or will attain can never be compared to the resources that God has made available for you.

The reason why your true worth is now beginning to show forth is because you are now beginning to function under the *direct magnetism* of heaven. When a magnet, no matter how small, is placed in a region with a large mound of soil with ferrous material in it, instead of the earth, soil or dirt controlling what goes on in that domain, the magnet takes over. The magnet has the power of attraction and it knows its own, which is the ferrous metal. The same thing happens with distinction of power. The magnet of heaven is able to locate you wherever you are, and you become distinct. You have become attractive to heaven and heaven has to do something about your situation. The same way that Jesus stood still when Blind Bartimaeus shouted, heaven will stand to attention waiting for your next command in Jesus' name, amen.

> Regarding Zion, I can't keep my mouth shut, regarding Jerusalem, I can't hold my tongue, Until her righteousness blazes down like the sun and her salvation flames up like a torch. Yes! God has broadcast to all the world:"Tell daughter Zion, "Look! Your Savior comes,Ready to do what he said he'd do, prepared to complete what he promised.' Zion will be called new names: Holy People, God-Redeemed,Sought-Out, City-Not-Forsaken. (Isaiah 62:1,11–12, MSG)

The statements as mentioned by the prophet Isaiah and Apostle Paul in the book of first Corinthians chapter 2:9 is the prepackaged and infallible Word of God wrapped up in time. "Your best is yet to come" does not mean that God has not "finished gloriously" everything that concerns you, but it just means you have to accept the dispensation of grace, propagate the dimension of establishment, provoke the displacement of principalities and applaud the distinction of power. One of the most confounding and mind boggling discussions that has "tko'ed" many eminent scholars and has prevented religious luminaries from shedding the toga of religion is the mystery of Godliness.

> And without controversy great is the mystery of godliness: God was manifest in the flesh, justified in the Spirit, seen of angels, preached unto the Gentiles, believed on in the world, received up into glory. (1 Timothy 3:16, KJV)

A declaration came from God in the book of Genesis that the seed of the woman will bruise the head of the serpent. Since then Satan has become homeless. He tried to stop Moses, David and even Jesus. Throughout the time of Jesus on earth, Satan was always trying to bring Him down. When he succeeded in convincing Judas Iscariot to decamp, he thought he had won. Satan did not know the best of Jesus was yet to come. No matter what has been thrown at you—loss of your spouse, disappointment by friends, loss of your job, a child becoming wayward—I want to tell you your best is yet to come. You shall be great.

> None of the rulers of this age or world perceived and recognized and understood this, for if they had, they would never have crucified the Lord of glory. (1 Corinthians 2:8, TAB)

YOUR PROBLEM DOES NOT EQUAL THE PROMISES OF GOD.

The word "problem" is taken from a Greek word called *proballein*. This means "throw before" or "put forward." Whatever is called a problem that you are facing is put before you to throw you forward. The problems came so that the promises of God can come to physical manifestation. When Joseph had a dream about being the head, because he knew in part, his immediate family also came to a hasty conclusion about the meaning of the dream. He was then sold into slavery. Little did they realize that the designated place for the realization of the dream was not their immediate vicinity. It was not a local but global dream.

> Thou shalt be over my house, and according unto thy word shall all my people be ruled: only in the throne will I be greater than thou. And Pharaoh said unto Joseph, See, I have set thee over all the land of Egypt.
> (Genesis 41:40–41, KJV)

YOU CAN STILL BECOME THE UNANIMOUS CHOICE

The proof of your relevance begins when members of your sphere of influence begin to confess your headship. It is always a monumental task for the members of your family to agree on one thing, or in this case to make the younger the mother. The Word of God already recognized that the members of one's household will be one's greatest enemy. Rebekah moved from sister to mother, and her generations yet unborn were blessed.

> And they blessed Rebekah, and said unto her, Thou art our sister, be thou the mother of thousands of millions, and let thy seed possess the gate of those which hate them.
> (Genesis 24:60, KJV)

YOU HAVE NOT SEEN ANYTHING YET

There is no limit to the elevations that God can bring about in the life of a man, no matter your humble location. The determining factor is what He has decided to do. Before God says it, He first thinks about it. The thinking about it involves a thorough process that involves fine-tuning and admiring with commensurate accolades for His finished work. The future (indefinite time to come) cannot hold back what God had purposed to do because He is the future. He only has to say it and it becomes reality. David was a man that God picked from the wilderness and raised above his siblings (1 Samuel 16:13), but instead of the anointing taking him to the throne, it paved the way for tribulations. When he finally became a king over vagabonds (1 Samuel 22:1–2), his joy was unleashed. Then began a progression from being king over Judah (2 Samuel 2:4) to all of Israel (2 Samuel 5:1–3) and finally being called the father of Jesus:

> And many charged him that he should hold his peace: but he cried the more a great deal, Thou son of David, have mercy on me. (Mark 10:48, KJV)

YOUR LATTER WILL BE GREATER THAN THE PAST

It is not always about how you start, but how you end. Though you are facing challenges today, it does not mean you will not become a champion tomorrow.

> So the LORD blessed the latter end of Job more than his beginning: for he had fourteen thousand sheep, and six thousand camels, and a thousand yoke of oxen, and a thousand she asses. (Job 42:12, KJV)

GOD RESERVES THE BEST FOR THE LAST

At the marriage in Cana of Galilee, the master of ceremony noted that the best wine had been left for the last, contrary to what normally happens in other wedding ceremonies. What made that occasion special was the presence of Jesus Christ. The presence of Jesus in your life has made you a special person. It is not over concerning you. The wine will not run dry.

> This Temple is going to end up far better than it started out, a glorious beginning but an even more glorious finish: a place [home] in which I will hand out wholeness and holiness.' Decree of God-of-the-Angel-Armies.
> (Haggai 2:9, MSG)

No matter your age or situation, it is not too late for you to take action. Greatness is according to what you do. It is time for you to meaningfully invest, progressively increase, wisely initiate, introspectively insight, stoically shrug of insult, morally be a person of integrity, diligently inquire and powerfully impact.

Now Go.
-Sept 13th 2022
Day 230